THE
WEIGHT
LIFTED

THE
WEIGHT
LIFTED

How the Cubs ended the longest drought in sports history

PAUL SULLIVAN

$\mathfrak{Chicago\ Tribune}$

MIDWAY

AN AGATE IMPRINT

CHICAGO

The Weight Lifted
ISBN 13: 978-1-57284-250-2
ISBN 10: 1-57284-250-4
eISBN 13: 978-1-57284-503-9
3ISBN 10: 1-57284-503-1

Printed in the United States of America

Chicago Tribune: R. Bruce Dold, Publisher & Editor-in-Chief; Peter Kendall, Managing Editor; Colin McMahon, Associate Editor; Amy Carr, Associate Managing Editor/Features; Joe Knowles, Associate Managing Editor/Sports.

10 9 8 7 6 5 4 3 2 1

Midway Books is an imprint of Agate Publishing. Agate books are available in bulk at discount prices. For more information, visit agatepublishing.com.

Contents

About this Book

Chicago Tribune baseball writer Paul Sullivan chronicled the Chicago Cubs 2016 championship season in 16 chapters, written as the season actually unfolded, starting with spring training in Arizona and ending in Cleveland with Game 7 of the World Series.

CHAPTER ONE
THE BEST-LAID PLANS

Originally published April 4, 2016

O N THE EVE of what's expected to be a momentous season, the Cubs tried to keep calm and carry on.

They'd been answering questions about great expectations for seven weeks in the Arizona desert.

Starting Monday night at Angel Stadium, they were eager to assure everyone it was just business as usual.

"Playing for a team like St. Louis where they expect to go to the playoffs every year and they expect to win every year, this is no different," new right fielder Jason Heyward said with the smoothness of Isaac Hayes. "Other than they haven't done it in a while."

No, they have not done it in a while. One hundred and seven years, to be exact.

"Just One Before I Die," read the royal blue T-shirt of a Cubs fan watching Sunday's final exhibition game.

"The Year" is here, and anything less than a trip to the World Series would be deemed unacceptable to the masses back home in Chicago.

"Hey, that's what their job is in this whole deal," newcomer Ben Zobrist said. "They get to do that."

Theo Epstein, left, Chicago Cubs president of baseball operations, and Chicago Cubs manager Joe Maddon, before their opening day game against the Los Angeles Angels, at Angel Stadium, in Anaheim, Calif. on April 4, 2016. *(Nuccio DiNuzzo/Chicago Tribune)*

How did we get to this point, where one group of men had the enormous weight of failure on their collective shoulders?

It all goes back to the summer of 2011, when there was no light at the end of this long, grinding tunnel. Unlovable losers? Yes, the 2011 Cubs were a miserable bunch, and an expensive one.

The only solution was the nuclear option, and the man with his finger on the button was Tom Ricketts, a nouveau owner whose entire wardrobe seemed to consist of tan khakis and light blue cotton shirts.

When the Ricketts family took control of the Cubs a year earlier, it entrusted Tom with the job of running the operation. He had no prior skills in the business and mostly stayed out of the baseball department's way.

But now it was all on Tom to find the right executive to make the Cubs relevant again.

In a Shakespearean twist, a thousand miles away, Theo Epstein was facing a Waterloo of his own. The fresh-faced, local hero who was at the wheel when the Red Sox ended their 86-year championship drought was now fighting with his bosses after a stunning stretch-run collapse knocked the Red Sox out of a playoff spot.

The Red Sox were only too happy to let Epstein seek employment elsewhere.

So when Ricketts offered him the title of president of baseball operations and the chance to rebuild the franchise the way he saw fit, the marriage was quickly consummated. No shotgun necessary.

The baseball-addicted city of Chicago, or at least the natives who didn't grow up White Sox fans, responded to the news of Epstein's hiring as one might expect. "Cautiously optimistic" was not in anyone's vocabulary.

Epstein was seen as the man who finally was going to bring them what they'd been seeking their entire lives. The Chicago Sun-Times featured a front-page illustration of Epstein walking on Lake Michigan.

Epstein, a Yale grad with a preppy outer shell hiding a wry sense of humor, took over the Cubs and wowed everyone in his opening news conference, talking about "parallel fronts" and "supply-and-demand dynamics." Epstein didn't know it then, but he had them at "information management systems."

This was not the jargon Cubs fans were used to hearing, and it was sweet music to their ears.

"Cultural changes don't come easily," Epstein announced. "You can't fake them. You have to do it through hard work. We're ready to do that."

After 103 years of losing, changing the Cubs' culture was certainly going to take some time. But the purge began almost immediately.

Players came and went. Free agents were signed and flipped for prospects. Waiver claims were made, and sometimes the same player would be waived a few days later.

The revolving door kept spinning, the losses piled up and waiting for the young talent to make its way through the farm system became the focus. Just when some were growing impatient with the lousy product on the field, a stroke of good fortune changed everything. A post-season debacle by the Dodgers in 2014 cost general manager Ned Colletti his job, and when Rays general manager Andrew Friedman was hired in Los Angeles, it triggered an out clause in Rays manager Joe Maddon's contract.

Voila. The last piece of the Cubs' puzzle was theirs for the taking.

Epstein and his wingman, general manager Jed Hoyer, swooped in and manager-jacked Maddon while the Rays owner napped. The two jetted down to Florida like Crockett and Tubbs going undercover to snare their man.

They met Maddon in his RV at Navarre Beach in Pensacola, gave him the lowdown on The Plan and offered him a fistful of dollars to bolt the Rays.

Between sipping cocktails and enjoying a beautiful Florida sunset, they signed Maddon to a five-year deal and jettisoned their current manager, whose only crime was not being Joe Maddon.

Once again, Cubs fans reacted with glorious understatement. A new savior had arrived, and no, his name was not Dusty.

Maddon quickly won the hearts and minds of Chicago by offering to buy a shot and a beer for everyone at his opening news conference at the Cubby Bear. He drank from a Guinness tall boy, and unlike one of his predecessors, admitted he had a streak of lunacy in him.

"You have to have a little bit of crazy to be successful," Maddon said. "I want crazy in the clubhouse every day. You need to be crazy to be great. I love crazy. I tell my players that all the time."

Maddon promised he would be "talking playoffs" the next year, bold talk for any new manager, much less someone taking over a team as cursed as the Cubs.

But no one doubted him. The Cubs went on to have a season to remember, winning 97 games, beating the Pirates in the wild-card game and trouncing their hated rivals, the Cardinals, in the division series.

When they were swept by the bleeping Mets—always the bleeping Mets—in the National League Championship Series, there was no gnashing of teeth or pointing of fingers at the team's inadequacies, as happened after similar playoff sweeps in 2007 and '08.

The better team had won, but the first big step of the journey had been completed.

There would be no more sneaking up on the world. The Cubs had arrived, and there was no turning back.

On Dec. 8, 2015, when focus-challenged infielder Starlin Castro was traded to the Yankees for pitcher Adam Warren, the turnover was complete. Every player from the 25-man roster Epstein inherited in 2011 was gone.

It was a stunning housecleaning, one that involved the eating of millions of dollars on the albatross contracts of Carlos Zambrano and Alfonso Soriano alone. Tom Ricketts swallowed the contracts with elan, understanding it was all in the name of a cultural cleansing.

If the Cubs' goal was to erase every memory of the old Cubs Way, they had succeeded. But as The Year everyone was waiting for neared, Epstein insisted a complete roster purge was not his original intent.

"If the team was good, we would've kept it," he said matter-of-factly during a spring training game at Sloan Park. "It wasn't by design. We've just been trying to add impact multidimensional players and we think probably the most talented players we inherited were Starlin and (starter Jeff) Samardzija.

"And we certainly tried to keep Samardzija and then ended up making what I thought was a pretty fair trade for him. With Starlin we did give him the contract and made some moves this winter where for us it made sense to turn Starlin into Warren and Zobrist, in essence.

"It certainly wasn't intentional, but we knew we'd be aggressive in trying to turn the franchise over. I've never thought about it in those terms. I just look at it as trying to get better as an organization."

A media tsunami hit Cubs camp at the start of spring training and never let up. Wave after wave of reporters ventured to Mesa, Ariz., to tell the tale of the team hoping to end the worst drought in sports history.

No one could escape it, and only a few of the players even tried. The boys in the Cubs bubble were suddenly in demand, and this quest for a championship was likely to be a crazy, hazy, head-shaking journey.

The weight of the many past disasters will follow these Cubs every step of the season, but they brought their blinders and ignored the win-or-else demands of the fans and media watching their every move.

"It comes with the territory," said first baseman Anthony Rizzo, the young Cubs slugger who looked like he came out of central casting. "And having all this media here will be better for us in the long run. The more the spotlight is on us now, the more we'll be used to it when the real spotlight is on us in the playoffs. Then it's just going to be normal."

Poor kid.

How was Rizzo supposed to know that nothing would ever be normal again?

Everything will be magnified now that the Cubs are seemingly on the doorstep of destiny. Chicago was just waiting for someone to kick the door in, and Epstein had chosen this wild bunch to go out and make history.

And now, let the wild rumpus start.

CHAPTER TWO
NO PLACE LIKE HOME
Originally published April 11, 2016

FOR MOST of the winter, the front entrance of Wrigley Field was covered in plastic like your grandma's couch.

Ugly as it looked, the protective cover was necessary to shield the construction workers from the Hawk wind that blew off Lake Michigan and into their bones. The wrap finally came off last week when the Cubs began to ready the park for the home opener, which arrives Monday night with the boys back in town.

Just as the revamped Cubs are loaded and ready to go after a 5-1 start to the season, the Cubs insist the still-under-construction ballpark will be ready for the packed house expected for the home opener.

Phase 2 of the renovation was a bit messy but productive. A new clubhouse is ready, and the free-range players are geeked about the possibility of moving around without bumping into someone from the fourth estate.

Phase 1 was marred by construction delays and an opening-night bathroom malfunction that eventually forced the Cubs to line the concourse with port-a-potties.

The tunnel that connects the Cubs new clubhouse with the dugout at Wrigley Field. The old, cramped clubhouse was gone, replaced by a 30,000-square-foot room that's bigger than anyone else's but the Yankees. *(John J. Kim/Chicago Tribune)*

Despite the many changes, Wrigley 2.0 will still be as beloved as the original, which is why it remains the gold standard of ballparks.

"It's the history," said David Ross, the gray-bearded catcher who won a ring with the Red Sox at Fenway Park. "I love going in there and feeling the energy. Old ballparks, the fans are right on top of you, and the green. ... For me, all the old, faded green, I love it.

"I love the tight quarters. It just feels like baseball. You're crammed into this little bitty dugout at Wrigley. Some people complain. I love it. You get to know your teammates, and everybody's cheering, and nobody lets anybody slide.

"Big dugouts seem empty sometimes."

The dugout will be sufficiently cramped on opening day. Nothing new there. It will be ready for the sunflower-seed showers players get after big home runs, the rhythmic clapping during someone's walk-up song, and the other shenanigans that make the Cubs the Cubs.

But the old, cramped clubhouse is gone, replaced by a 30,000-square-foot room that's bigger than anyone else's but the Yankees, the team from New York that serves as a Bizarro World version of the Cubs.

The new clubhouse, built underground below an old parking lot on the west side of the ballpark, has only been seen by a few. President Theo Epstein wanted his crew to be the first to gaze upon its majesty, like Dorothy and her posse getting their first glimpse of Oz after the long journey down the yellow brick road.

"You guys know what the old clubhouse was like," Chairman Tom Ricketts said. "It's night and day. It's incredible."

The Cubs never won a championship in the old clubhouse at Wrigley, or the one before it. Not once in a century have they won, so perhaps the antiquated ballpark was part of the reason for all those dismal decades.

"I don't know about that," pitcher Jason Hammel countered. "They've had good teams here in the past. For whatever reason, finishing the job in October has been the problem. I don't think it has anything to do with the (lack of amenities)."

No matter the reason, change has arrived. The consigliere of the clubhouse is a balding, middle-aged man who goes by the name of Otis, though his given name is Tom Hellmann. Otis is the longtime clubhouse manager, with 33 years in the organization, starting on the visitors' side before replacing the legendary Yosh Kawano in the '90s.

Players spend half their lives in clubhouses. It's their home away from home, and they expect to feel at home, except without their kids asking them for a juice box and some microwaved mac and cheese. Going from the cozy, old clubhouse to the super-sized version is going to be an adjustment, but one Otis feels will be welcomed like the first robin in spring.

"The difference? I was there when we went from no lights to lights," Otis said, referring to the Cubs' submission to night baseball at Wrigley Field on Aug. 8, 1988. "Let's put it that way."

The old clubhouse, under the stands behind the dugout, debuted in 1984, a dividing line in Cubs history. The previous clubhouse was located down the left-field line, where Ron Santo would jump up and click his heels en route to the postgame spread. The visitors' side remains a shoebox, though they did change from metal lockers in 1990 when the Cubs were awarded the All-Star Game.

The visitors will have to wait until the final phase of the renovation project to get their much-needed space.

Otis assigns the lockers for Cubs players, making him the unofficial director of clubhouse feng shui. You don't want to put the wrong players next to each other and risk upsetting the clubhouse chemistry. Notorious malcontent Milton Bradley, for instance, was placed next to happy-go-lucky Cajun Ryan Theriot, who didn't blink the day Bradley cashed a paycheck and stacked his money in his locker for everyone to see.

But Otis let the veterans pick their own lockers this year so they can choose which friends they want to kibitz with on a daily basis. The coaches and clubhouse men and others who don't actually play will dress in different rooms, meaning the players finally have the joint to themselves for the first time in a century.

Since the clubhouse is round instead of rectangular, the so-called "crazy locker" in the corner is gone, never to return. It was inhabited by Carlos Zambrano, Matt Garza, Carlos Villanueva and Grandpa Ross in recent years, thus the name. It's whereabouts are unknown.

The clubhouse was particularly a treat on getaway day, when duffel bags full of uniforms, clothes and equipment were strewn all over the floor as players showered and dressed and the media congregated at lockers waiting for the bon mots. It often resembled a game of Twister played by squirrels.

"We had to make it work," Otis said. "And we did. This place is going to be so much nicer. Long time coming. It's so nice, I don't know how much they'll hang out at their lockers. There are so many other places to go. It'll be a trial-and-error type of thing, see where they hang out. They'll hide from the media."

Ross concurred with Otis. No one will be hanging out much in the spacious quarters.

"There will be a little bit more luxury," Ross said. "But I have a feeling we'll be tucked away in a little-bitty room somewhere, knowing us."

Still, some of the old standbys will be missed. Hammel joked he would miss the rats, the ones former White Sox manager Ozzie

Guillen often referred to when describing Wrigley as a "dump." Hammel confirmed Guillen's stories are not the stuff of urban legend.

"The rats were mostly in the storage areas back behind where the lockers are," he said. "But one thing I won't miss, if and when we're celebrating, is I won't have a puddle of booze puddled up in front of my locker. There were some low spots in the old clubhouse."

Whether the humongous new clubhouse will make a difference in the Cubs' performance on the field is a question no one can answer, even the man who is paying for the changes.

"I don't know," Ricketts said. "I hope so, though we did pretty well last year with the old clubhouse. What it can do is the players will have batting cages, we'll have a better weight room, we'll have different aqua therapy, we'll have room for the Pilates reformers.

"It'll be a better place for them to be prepared for the game, which I think ultimately could lead to some more success. But I don't know how you quantify it."

Hammel believes bigger will be better. He pointed to the old contraption that dropped a net out of the ceiling like something out of "Get Smart," acting as a poor man's batting cage for players who needed to take some swings before an in-game at-bat.

"With as far as this game has come along, technology and stuff, it's a necessary evil," he said. "It's stuff we have to have in a stadium that's pretty old and has a lot of rings on its tree. We've got to have some updates, and I think everyone is welcoming it."

The option of cutting down the old tree and planting a new one was always there for the Rickettses. Even before they bought the Cubs, the franchise had spent an inordinate amount of time over the last few decades fighting with the city and the neighbors over how they should run their business.

It probably would've been easier to move to a generic suburb like Rosemont and build a spanking new park with all the modern amenities and doodads and who-has.

But home is home, and truth be told, there is no place quite like Wrigley Field.

Warts and all, it's still the place of your daydreams.

CHAPTER THREE
THE RIVALRY

Originally published April 21, 2016

THE STORIED 124-YEAR-OLD RIVALRY, the one that gave us Brock for Broglio, the Ryno Game and the Great Home Run Race of 1998, resumed at Busch Stadium with a classical music soundtrack, a T-shirt controversy and a chance for the Cubs to make an early statement.

President Theo Epstein predicted in spring training that beating the Cardinals the way the Cubs did in October would be "transformative," and this was their first opportunity to see if the tide had actually turned.

After Wednesday's 5-3 loss to the Cardinals, the Cubs wound up taking two of three, one small step in April they hope will reverberate in September.

"You want to win series in your division," said Cardinals refugee Jason Heyward, the Cubs right fielder who received St. Louis' undivided attention every time he stepped to the plate.

"That's big time. It affects the standings right away. What we're doing right now is going to work in our favor for later in the season, when it can come down to one game."

The Cubs-Cardinals rivalry is one of the best in baseball.
(Nuccio DiNuzzo/Chicago Tribune)

There was little doubt the Cubs had moved into the high-rent district after decades of looking up at the smaller-city team with the best pedigree in the National League.

For years here they have worshiped at the altar of Branch Rickey, lauding the genius of George "The Professor" Kissell, the architect of the "Cardinals Way" of playing baseball. It was injected like truth serum into every player and coach in the system and hyped as though the franchise had invented fundamentals.

When you win as much as the Cardinals have, you are entitled to have a "Way." But the Cubs flipped the script in 2012, when Epstein and his wingmen wrote their own manifesto, the "Cubs Way."

A Cubs Way? The brass practically invited mocking from the media by being so confident their plan would succeed. The Cubs, of course, were the sad sacks who never got the girl. The "Cubs Way" sounded as weird as the "Edsel Way" or the "Pharma Bro Way." How could it possibly measure up to the Cardinals Way?

"Every great organization has a way of doing things, going back to the Dodger Way and their great stability," said general manager Jed Hoyer, Epstein's lieutenant and BFF. "They had the Dodger Way of teaching and then the Oriole Way. The Cardinal Way has gotten a lot of attention, and it should. They've done a great job teaching fundamentals and in player development.

"Ultimately that's the way we see it: teaching our players how to play fundamentally and how we want them to play."

The series kicked off with Heyward giving a thoughtful explanation of why he left the Cardinals as a free agent after one season before it evolved into a discussion of the massive T-shirt collection Cubs players have gotten from manager Joe Maddon and the coaches.

Besides the ubiquitous "Try Not to Suck" and "Embrace the Target" shirts Maddon favors, several other customized T-shirts were on display, including one from the mental-skills department of a bear in a yoga position.

On this comfortable afternoon, Heyward wore one depicting a cartoon bull with a Cubs logo on it, suggesting a "take the bull by the horns" motif.

"This is one of, like, 15 so far," Heyward said. "So it's early. This may be the weight room or the mental-skills one. I don't know which one."

The Cubs took the opener behind seven shutout innings from another Cardinals refugee, John Lackey, whose teeth were so white you could see them from atop the Arch. They brought their dance party to the visitors clubhouse afterward while Maddon enjoyed a glass of red wine in his office.

Millennials new to this Cubs-Cardinals thing might have had no idea these ancient NL franchises with so much bad blood between them once had very distinct personalities, like Taylor Swift and Katy Perry.

The Cubs were a day-baseball, mascot-averse, video-free, Harry Caray-oke, Old Style kind of experience. The Cardinals were night games, Fredbird, Kiss-Cam, Jack Buck and Bud—the beer, not the commissioner.

But the Cubs have made Wrigley Field much more Busch-like in recent years. A massive Budweiser sign was erected in right field, and the corporate giant also bought naming rights to the bleachers while Old Style became the forgotten stepchild of Wrigley.

A humorless, pantsless, costumed bear named Clark now roams the ballpark like he owns it, and from Tribune Co. to the Ricketts family, Cubs owners gradually abandoned more of the day-game tradition for the sake of TV revenues.

Likewise, the Cardinals quietly have begun emulating the Cubs. After decades of playing in the generic saucer that was old Busch Stadium, a place where you would feel like you spent a day inside a microwave turned to the popcorn setting, they built a new, red-brick Busch 10 years ago with Wrigley's early 20th-century charm in mind.

Then the Cardinals unapologetically borrowed the Wrigleyville concept of rooftop parties, erecting a bar/restaurant with rooftop seats outside the left-field wall. And when the Cubs added giant video boards last year, the Cardinals kept up with the Rickettses by getting a bigger one for themselves.

As red-and-blue-clad fans began to cram into Busch for Game 2, Hoyer announced that Kyle Schwarber had undergone successful knee surgery in Dallas while Anthony Rizzo walked around the clubhouse with a jewelry box "borrowed" from Ben Zobrist's locker.

Inside the box was Zobrist's World Series ring from the Royals, which he had received earlier in the day. Rizzo popped it open like Julia Roberts in "Pretty Woman," dreaming of the day he would have one of his own to show off.

Perhaps inspired by Zobrist's new bling, the Cubs edged the Cardinals 2-1 to clinch the series. The atmosphere on this summerlike night was electric and winning pitcher Jason Hammel felt the vibe from the first pitch.

"What is it, Game 11 or 12 or something like that? And it's already heated," Hammel said afterward. "This is the best rivalry in baseball. The rivalry goes back a long time and you always have good ballgames. Neither team is out of it just because of the energy the crowd brings."

Maddon, with a new bottle of wine on his desk, set a later club-house arrival time for the next morning, giving his players a chance to catch up on sleep on getaway day.

But the usual suspects still arrived early, such as catcher David Ross, the OG (Original Grandpa), who yelled at coach Gary Jones: "Jonesy, gotta have it!"

The two clubhouse TVs were muted before Game 3, one showing MLB Network and the other a "Leave it to Beaver" rerun. The joint was dead silent when Rizzo walked in with a stoic look.

Suddenly, the song "I Want to be Your Lady Baby" by INOJ was playing full blast and Rizzo began dancing. Dexter Fowler emerged from behind a pole laughing, having waited for Rizzo's arrival to see if the song would make him dance.

Maddon was also in the mood for mischief and addressed the tempest-in-a-T-shirt scandal, relaying a story he had heard from a Cubs fan that Busch Stadium ushers banned the "Try Not to Suck" shirts, saying they were offensive.

"The message to the ushers is, 'Why do you think it's dirty?'" Maddon said, grinning like the Cheshire Cat.

The psychological warfare had begun.

Whether this first Cubs-Cardinals series meant anything or not, the Cubs were feeling frisky. It all started here in October and has continued unabated into April.

"I do think now when we come in here, there's a feeling we have the ability to play with them," Hoyer said. "Our ability to do that over a long period of time will kind of determine our success.

"But I do feel like winning a playoff series against them probably gave our guys a lot of confidence that it's a real rivalry now."

CHAPTER FOUR
THE PIRATES

Originally published May 8, 2016

THE CUBS STARTED the season with great expectations and exceeded them in the first month, taking the pole position in the National League Central race and ignoring the ruckus in the rearview mirror.

Only a couple of years earlier, you wondered how the Cubs ever won a game. Suddenly it felt weird to see them lose.

"Does it feel weird? No," argued Kris Bryant, the third baseman moonlighting as an outfielder. "We realize we're not going to win every game, but we do have that confidence in that every time we walk in this clubhouse, we believe we're going to win every game. That's the right one to have."

That was why the first trip to Pittsburgh was so appetizing to manager Joe Maddon after what felt like a week off against the Brewers and Braves. The Cubs had handled the Cardinals two of three at Busch Stadium and now returned to the scene of their wild-card triumph, where a brouhaha had erupted, as brouhahas tend to do.

More shenanigans were on the docket. The Pirates have the best hitting in the majors. The Cubs were throwing their three hottest starters. And no one tried to pretend it wasn't important to establish

"There's no false sense of humility," Joe Maddon said of pitcher Jake Arrieta. "He's a very self-confident person, and I like that."
(Anthony Souffle/Chicago Tribune)

an identity in what everyone figured was a three-way runoff that includes the Cardinals.

"During the course of a major-league season, when you get into that point when you're doing well and you play other teams that are doing well, it really makes for an interesting evening, and I love that," Maddon said before the trip. "I think our players feel the same way. It's something to look forward to."

To get his players relaxed and prepared, Maddon called for one of his patented theme trips, the first since Jake Arrieta threw a no-hitter nine months earlier in Los Angeles, then wore a onesie to his news conference.

The team dressed in "zany suits" of colorful patterns and prints, trying to one-up each other with their boldness. Bullpen coach Les Strode sang on the plane "because he looked so hot," Maddon revealed, and everyone posed for the obligatory yearbook shot.

Reliever Clayton Richard wore a Riddler get-up from "Batman" that Maddon boasted was "above and beyond" the call of duty. Still, it was unclear if Richard was impersonating Frank Gorshin's Riddler or Jim Carrey's Riddler.

"Is Frank Gorshin the guy from the TV show?" Richard asked. "Was that in the 1970s?"

Sixties? Seventies? It was all ancient history to this bunch.

Gorshin was the original Riddler on the 1960s TV show, with a cackle that can't be replicated. Richard wasn't alive then but had watched the show in reruns as a kid.

"It's more Gorshin because the costume shop had that available for the jacket and hat," he said. "There were dual images. I wanted to give the spirit of the costume. It worked out perfectly. Had an awkward walk over to the park."

No matter. The mood was properly set. The Cubs looked like a million bucks, and it was time to find out if they were dressed for success.

The series opener picked up where the wild-card game left off, with the Cubs jumping to a lead before the fun really began. Obscure Pirates reliever Kyle Lobstein plunked serial nice guy Ben Zobrist leading off the seventh inning, leading to a profane response from Maddon.

The f-bombs flew faster than a Ferrari on Fullerton and were duly caught on video and disseminated by amateur lip readers back in Chicago. Maddon's friends confirmed it was the angriest they had seen him since he left the Rays.

Secretly, Maddon was beaming. The old-school side of him prefers a rivalry that grows "organically," free of the preservatives that define the typical hate-fests based on proximity or longevity.

An organic rivalry comes out of nowhere and escalates quickly, fueled by the media, social media and mostly by the players and managers in the middle. Maddon was certain now that this rivalry was organically grown and ready for consumption.

Postgame interviews are usually short and sweet, but Maddon's presser was Fellini-esque. As President Theo Epstein sat in the corner of the cramped visiting manager's office checking his iPhone, Maddon emoted. A half-empty glass and bottle of wine seemingly enhanced his Oscar-worthy performance. It was vintage Joe.

He rambled on about a variety of topics, including a Hazleton-West Hazleton football game in a snowstorm, the fact the Pirates uniform also was known as a "unigram" and the need for everyone to vent for health reasons. He admitted he challenged a slide for the sake of having some fun with the Pirates.

The f-bomb-apalooza had been cathartic.

"'Zorilla' was fine," Maddon said. "And I was able to vent a little bit."

Zorilla was Zobrist, who also answered to "Zo" and "Zobi Wan Kenobi." Zobrist is such a genial fellow he probably would respond if you called him "the Zobrinator," "Zo Slamma Jamma" or "Thus Spoke Zorathustra."

Zorilla's response to the purpose pitch was not exactly threatening.

"I hope they feel good about it," Zobrist said. "It was an earned run for them. I know I feel good about it. That's it."

So be it. The Cubs felt good about their victory, especially considering Jason Heyward was out with a sore wrist and Arrieta was going the next day. But the following morning the Cubs announced Matt Szczur was headed to the disabled list with a strained hamstring, leaving them two outfielders down.

"Bad timing," said Szczur, who had spent most of 2015 shuttling back and forth between the Cubs and Triple-A Iowa. Szczur, the ultimate grinder, finally had begun to make an impact in a reserve role, hitting .367 and driving in 10 runs in only 34 at-bats.

"The last step for him was for him to realize he belongs in the major leagues and he could do this," Maddon said. "You could hear it conversationally. He talks differently. He's more confident."

Partial credit for that confidence went to a rock, specifically a touchstone that rested on a shelf in Szczur's locker at Wrigley Field. After his first career grand slam helped beat the Braves a few days before the zany-suit trip, Szczur said it was from his family's old restaurant and related to a parable called "the Stonecutter," which he had learned from a priest while playing football at Villanova University.

After trying to break a stone by tapping it for a long time, the stonecutter finally cracked it with a tap. The moral was that it was not the final tap that broke the stone, but all the collective taps beforehand.

"That reminds me every day, keep grinding," he said.

Szczur heeded the lesson and touched the rock before games. But the grind was put on hold, as baseball waits for no one.

In Szczur's place came another typecast grinder, former Cubs outfielder Ryan Kalish, who had been out of the game and chilling at his Venice, Calif., home since leaving the organization after the 2014 season.

Epstein and Jason McLeod had drafted Kalish for the Red Sox in the ninth round in 2006, but injuries and inconsistency plagued his career. While unemployed in Venice, the surfer dude said some of his closest friends advised him to move on with his life.

He wouldn't listen. Kalish was ready to sign with an independent league team in Sioux City, Iowa, when the Cubs handed him a minor-league deal in March. Now he was back with the Cubs, and back with Anthony Rizzo, his teammate in Class A ball in Greenville, S.C., when Rizzo learned he had cancer.

"It was good for all of us to see," Kalish recalled, "because you just never know how long this is all going to last. For me, it's really cool to be here with him as well. We came up so long ago together, and he's doing such an incredible job."

Kalish didn't have a zany suit in Iowa, so he borrowed a jacket with several skulls printed on it from Arrieta, who brought a spare zany suit just in case. In the second game of the series, Arrieta dominated the Pirates over seven shutout innings for his 17th straight victory, and the Cubs cruised again.

The dominance was so expected from Arrieta, there were no superlatives left for Maddon to utter.

"He's the same guy," Maddon said. "There's no false sense of humility. He's a very self-confident person, and I like that."

Arrieta proved that moments later. Informed the only reason Matt Joyce was put in the lineup was his numbers against Arrieta earlier in their careers, the pitcher responded: "Well, he's facing a different guy now. So it's a different story."

The Cubs slept fast, and getaway-day morning was quiet and contemplative, at least until Rizzo arrived fashionably late in his star-spangled jacket and red shorts, looking like a refugee from a Lynyrd Skynyrd concert.

Bryant and hitting coach John Mallee studied video together. Jorge Soler sat on a couch and played a video game on his iPad. David Ross sang "What's Love Got to Do With It?" in the wrong key, while Maddon ate oatmeal in his office while cranking up Simon & Garfunkel's "America."

It was up to Jon Lester to seal the sweep, and seal it he did. He also made the play of the day, grabbing a comebacker and throwing his glove to Rizzo when he couldn't get the ball out of the webbing.

Rizzo dropped his own glove to catch Lester's, a reprise of the glove story that made every "SportsCenter" telecast over a 24-hour stretch last season.

"And didn't Anthony drop his glove the last time we did that also?" Maddon asked knowingly. "OK, we have that down too. And the cradling of the glove! The glove was cradled perfectly."

Lester was the old Lester again. Silencing chatter about his fielding may be his biggest challenge remaining.

In his previous start, Lester ate a comebacker to load the bases. Lester explained he had bobbled the ball in his glove and didn't want to risk throwing it away. Maddon coined a new euphemism, suggesting Lester was "taking a sack."

Lester's issue throwing to bases had been well-chronicled. Though he had worked on the problem in spring training, Lester realized he always would be presumed guilty of being afraid to make a throw.

"The frustrating part for me is I try to be honest and truthful with everybody," he said. "I'm not hiding from anything. And it's still an issue. It didn't matter what I said about it. Nobody knows what actually happened in my glove other than me."

Even though Lester escaped the jam, allowing one run over seven innings and striking out 10 in a Cubs triumph, a national media outlet insisted "the sack" overshadowed his victory.

"I sit there and answer the questions as truthfully as I can," Lester said. "People write what they want, and I'll just try to get better at it and try to pitch as well as I can. That's all I can do."

Lester's earned-run average shrank to 1.58, eighth in the majors, so no one was fretting his throwing issue, at least for the moment.

The Cubs dressed up one last time for the flight home, secure in the knowledge they had done their jobs and had a few laughs. Zaniness ruled.

"I had the idea and thought it would be good," Maddon said. "But I didn't know it was going to be this good. This was one of the best ever. Why? Because the guys totally bought in, man, and they took it to another level."

But there was no time to breathe.

Dusty Baker returned to Wrigley with the Nationals, and the Cubs were back on the clock.

CHAPTER FIVE
THE TRAVELING CIRCUS
Originally published May 24, 2016

IT WAS 32 MILES to Milwaukee, they had full tanks of gas and coolers full of beer. It was getting dark, and they were wearing prescription sunglasses and Cubs caps.

Occupy Miller Park was underway.

The Cubs were on the road again, and thousands of fully krausened, road-tripping fans flew past the Mars Cheese Castle on Interstate 94, ready to make themselves right at home in the world's largest garage with a retractable roof.

According to a Cubs source with inside knowledge of the road trippers, this year was destined to be a bull market for Cubs fans based on the surge of autograph seekers he had seen in the team's hotel lobbies.

"The opening series in Anaheim was crazy," said the source, who asked not to be identified. "Then came Arizona, where Cubs fans move to, so they always come out. Cincinnati had more than ever for this early in the season. Four years ago we arrived at the hotel in Cincy, and there was no one in the lobby at all.

Chicago Cubs fan Nicole Edwards of Antioch has her photograph taken with Cubs second baseman Ben Zobrist before a game against the Milwaukee Brewers at Miller Park in Milwaukee on May 18, 2016.
(Chris Sweda/Chicago Tribune)

"St. Louis was the usual (amount), though most of them don't know where we stay anymore. Pittsburgh ... and of course (Milwaukee), where they take over the ballpark. And once kids get out of school ..."

It was no surprise Cubs fans were following the team on the road. Gas prices were low, the Cubs had the best record in baseball, and as many explained, it was cheaper, and often easier, to get tickets in opponents' parks.

"It's awesome," said right fielder Jason Heyward, who had a similar experience in St. Louis. "That's what's pretty cool about this division. Fans can travel. Of course there are going to be more fans for the Cubs, Cardinals, Pirates on the road right now with how we're playing. But it's something you don't take for granted. I definitely don't."

The Brewers knew the invasion was inevitable. They also understood they could do nothing about it.

Craig Counsell, the "Wisconsin-nice" manager of the Brewers, did not feel the need to warn his new players of what was in store.

"Guys like big crowds," Counsell said. "Players love big crowds. They love big crowds. Every player wants to play in front of big crowds. These guys are performers, so big crowds, that's a great thing."

In case he didn't make it perfectly clear, Counsell was OK with the occupation. Left fielder Ryan Braun, the closest equivalent to Lord Voldemort in the eyes of Cubs fans, was accustomed to being booed in his home park.

"We're used to it now," Braun said. "Even when (the Cubs) were going through their rebuild, their fans traveled well and supported them wherever they were.

"Whether it's here, or spring training in Arizona or anywhere else on the road, they're an extremely loyal and passionate fan base. And being that it's only an hour or an hour and a half away (by car), we're certainly used to it feeling as much like a road game as a home game can be.

"It makes for a fun atmosphere. There should be a lot of energy because it should be more crowded when these guys are in town."

Jim Sanders, 72, and his 42-year-old son, Jeff, made a father-and-son trip from Yorkville to watch the Cubs open the Brewers series Tuesday night.

They were perched in the back row of section 223, having moved from seats close to the action because a young, female fan sitting near them would not stop swearing.

To the Sanderses, Wrigley is a great place to go in your mind, just not in your car.

"I don't like going to Wrigley," Jeff said. "It's too crowded, and I don't like driving into Chicago."

They already had planned to go to Cincinnati in June, hoping to schedule their next trip around a Jake Arrieta start. When they are not road-tripping, they prefer to watch the Cubs on TV.

"I would watch until they did something stupid," Jim said. "Now the other team does something stupid first. That shows the evolution of the Cubs."

Most Cubs fans, like 81-year-old Fred Harnisch of the Hegewisch neighborhood on the far South Side of Chicago, say they cherish Wrigley.

"But it's a lot easier to get tickets (in Milwaukee)," Harnisch explained.

So Harnisch and 79-year-old buddy Ken Nelson drove up for the series, stayed at a local casino hotel, lost at bingo and ventured out to Miller Park for a Cubs fix.

There appeared to be slightly more Cubs fans than Brewers followers for the opener, judging from the shades of blue in the stands. But they didn't have much to cheer about when someone named Chase Anderson no-hit the Cubs through seven innings.

When Ben Zobrist broke up the no-no with a double leading off the eighth, the silent majority finally erupted.

Had Zobrist ever seen a home crowd cheer the break-up of its starter's no-hitter?

"Uh, no," Zobrist chuckled. "I've been a part of some no-hitters in my time in Tampa Bay. It was interesting. It's definitely home away from home, obviously, with the crowd we had up here. It's a pretty cool experience seeing that.

"I usually have been on the other end of that. We had times when the Yankees or the Red Sox would come down to Tampa Bay and it was tough to hear our crowd sometimes. It's nice to be on the other side. Cubs fans travel really well, so it's cool."

The Cubs were in dire need of an energy infusion Wednesday night, so manager Joe Maddon provided an eye-opener with a hot pink T-shirt with a flamingo on it and the phrase "If you look hot, wear it."

Maddon, a serial sloganeer, planned to showcase it for "Sunday Night Baseball" in San Francisco, the next stop on the trip. The T-shirts were for his charity, and Maddon was trying to raise enough money to provide him with more free time during the offseason.

"The thoughts are mine, and (the makers) design," he said. "I throw out my little things now and then, and they remind me they're the designers. You get so busy in your day job, or in your 'day-slash-night' job, I don't put as much mental time into it."

As the crowd filed back into Miller Park during Cubs batting practice, the parking lot was rife with tailgaters, some of whom ignored grilling and stuck to drinking. Inside, the ballpark had turned into a town hall meeting. Strangers in Cubs gear conversed in the concession lines like they all had carpooled together.

"It's Wrigley North," said Jane Rivi, a school nurse from Wilmette who drove up with her family. They had gone to Cleveland last year to watch the Cubs and had planned a trip to Cincinnati and Pittsburgh in September.

"It's easier to (come) here than to Wrigley, and I so love this ballpark," Rivi said. "I was feeling a little guilty last night that so many Cubs fans were here. I kind of felt sorry for the Brewers. But then we were almost no-hit. Now I just want to kick their butts."

In the highest level of the ballpark, 24-year-old John Doyle of Park Ridge stood in line at a card table where fans were allowed to make homemade signs. Wearing his Cubs cap backward, Doyle borrowed a Sharpie and wrote, "TRY NOT TO SUCK."

Only a few weeks earlier, Cubs fans in St. Louis had been asked to take off the ubiquitous "Try Not to Suck" shirts that ushers deemed offensive. Doyle knew there were no rules in Wisconsin, as evidenced by the state motto, "No Rules in Wisconsin."

"I just think it's funny that Joe is trying to instill this whole new culture," Doyle said. "Growing up with more than 100 years of losing, it pokes fun at Chicago's culture and also is saying, 'Yeah, it's time to step up.' It's funny to me the players themselves wear it. They understand the humor in it."

As starting pitcher John Lackey loosened up in the outfield before his bullpen session, 33-year-old Alonzo Flores and a buddy watched from a bar stool overlooking center field. Flores, from Racine, Wis., paid $1 for a so-called "Uecker seat" in the upper deck, named for popular Brewers broadcaster Bob Uecker.

Flores and his pal had no intention of watching their Cubs from the cheap seats. As soon as they got through the gate, they high-tailed it to center for the coveted bar stools.

"Sometimes I feel Brewers fans get annoyed with us," Flores said, referring to Cubs fans. "But, hey, go complain to ownership and get better."

Brewers general manager David Stearns, a fresh-faced 31-year-old who could be mistaken for the bat boy, was not annoyed by the influx of Cubs jerseys. He knew it was his job to change the ratio of Cubs fans to Brewers fans.

"We have to win more games," Stearns said. "The more games we win, the more Brewers fans are going to come to our park."

A larger crowd of 31,212 showed up for Game 2, and Cubsapalooza reigned again. The Cubs were forced to work overtime in their "day-slash-night" jobs. After being blanked for eight innings, they tied it up in the ninth and eventually won 2-1 in 13 innings.

By midnight, most of the Brewers fans had departed, leaving their counterparts to turn out the lights when the party was over.

The Cubs arrived bleary-eyed and weary the next morning for Thursday's day game, including the fashionably late Anthony Rizzo. David Ross, a morning person 24 hours a day, provided the only clubhouse noise.

Game 2 hero Travis Wood was also late, at least by his standards, arriving three hours before game time. Last summer during American Legion Week, when Maddon ordered the clubhouse door locked in the morning so players would not be tempted to show up early, Wood ignored the edict and stood outside the door until someone let him in.

What did Wood drink to wake up?

"Nothing," he said. "I don't drink a whole lot of coffee. I drink a Red Bull throughout the game, but other than that ... I've always been a get up early, get the day started (guy). Everyone knows they have a job to do. Get here, and put your game face on."

Maddon's game face was not yet locked and loaded when he met with the media before the series finale. He admitted he hardly had slept after drinking green tea during the intense game, then launched into a stream of consciousness on defunct ballparks.

"I was buzzing last night," Maddon said. "I was drinking it until about 12:30. I was lying in bed. Can't go to sleep. Watching YouTube (on) old ballparks. Shibe Park. Polo Grounds. Ebbets Field. Sportsman's Park. It was really cool stuff.

"It's a shame we haven't kept these ballparks and utilized them for city ventures, youth leagues. I hate going to Yankee Stadium and seeing the old Yankee Stadium gone. It's just not right. The Colosseum still exists in Rome."

Miller Park is no Colosseum, and the Cubs were no gladiators, losing the finale 5-3 before flying to San Francisco for a much-hyped series against the Giants.

The caravan of Cubs fans headed back home, their eyes on the road and their hands upon the wheel.

Let it roll, baby, roll.

CHAPTER SIX
THE MANAGERS

Originally published June 12, 2016

THE PRESSURE of trying to end the Cubs' drought took a toll on Dusty Baker. A decade and two managerial jobs later, the scars have yet to heal.

He brought them to within five outs of a World Series, closer than any manager has done over the last 71 years. But looking back on it now, in his first year as manager of the Nationals, Baker doesn't consider his time in Chicago a good experience.

"The Cubs? It's kind of a faint memory to me, especially when things don't end the way you want them to end," Baker said. "And the way I was booed at the end. Why would I try to remember that?"

But Baker never will get the Cubs out of his system, and many Cubs fans probably never will get him out of theirs. Once a conquering hero, Baker was the guy who would take them to the promised land. That didn't happen for various reasons, including dwindling resources from ownership that led to talent-challenged teams.

In '07, when the Cubs dipped into the coffers to sign free agents Alfonso Soriano, Ted Lilly and others after Lou Piniella had replaced Baker, the onetime savior could only shake his head.

Cubs manager Joe Maddon in the dugout at Wrigley Field. "I have to make up my own mind about things," Maddon said. "I'm not one to call up people and ask them about situations because it's how we react to stimulus that makes us all different." *(Nancy Stone/Chicago Tribune)*

"After I left they sunk millions into (the payroll)," Baker said. "For Lou, they were throwing away money. But, hey, I did the best I could.

"I wanted to be the guy. Maybe Joe is the guy. But I'm in the way now."

Maddon ridin' high

At the moment, Joe—as in Joe Maddon—had no worries and nothing much seemed to be in his way. He was the most popular Cubs manager in at least a generation, rivaling old friend Don Zimmer. His Cubs were on their six-month dress rehearsal for October.

Baker admitted Maddon's Cubs were the team to beat in the National League.

"Hey, man, I don't know what's going to happen here," he said. "All I know is Theo (Epstein) has put together a dynamite team through free agency, through trades, through the draft, through Latin America. They put together a heck of a team. They're the best team we've seen so far. But all our games were relatively close. They did get most of the breaks that series."

That was the four-game sweep in early May, and the breaks to which Baker referred included Anthony Rizzo's home run that touched the Ryne Sandberg flag on the foul pole and was ruled fair after Baker challenged the call, and Addison Russell's game-winning hit that Bryce Harper missed at the wall down the right-field line, and a hit by reliever Trevor Cahill.

"When you're going good, you get those things," he said. "Or when you're thinking positive, you get those things. But we'll see them again."

Yes, the Nationals would see the Cubs again. After the end of their last series at Turner Field in Atlanta, they would travel to Washington to begin another showdown with the Nats.

The big rematch

But that was not the series to which Baker was referring.

"Not only will we see them at our place," he said. "We'll see them at the end."

The playoffs?

"I think so," he said. "That's what I envision."

In the NLCS?

"Somewhere," he said.

Head games

Joe Maddon liked to play head games, that much we knew.

He did it last September against the Cardinals, calling them out for alleged "vigilantism" and setting the stage for an October showdown that vaulted the Cubs into the National League Championship Series.

And when the Nationals came to Wrigley Field in early May for a barometer series against the Cubs, full-metal Maddon was once again on display. This time Maddon decided to mess with the head of most valuable player Harper, and, through osmosis, Baker.

The Cubs walked Harper 13 times during their four-game sweep, including an MLB-record six times in the finale when the poster child for "Make Baseball Fun Again" received three intentional walks. Baker was not a fan of the strategy.

Maddon laughed it off, offering no apologies for trying to win.

Five weeks later, the Cubs prepared for a march on Washington, where Joe vs. Dusty would begin anew.

Managerial rivalries come and go, but this one already was getting interesting. As he prepared for a White Sox game a week before facing the Cubs, Baker was dismissive of the strategy, saying no other team had copied the approach.

"Not to that degree," Baker said. "That kind of started Bryce's fall at the time, kind of played with his patience. Now he's getting it back, swinging better, and maybe this side of Chicago will be kinder to him and to us than the other side of Chicago."

Harper hit .197 in his first 22 games after Maddon's head games.

If Maddon's move played with Harper's head, why didn't other teams try it?

"Nobody knew," Baker said. "Nobody knew it was going to play with his head that time. And there might be other teams that want to rise to the occasion and be competitive, you know? There are some teams that aren't running from Bryce, either. Not the last couple of weeks, at least."

Baker admitted he has said to himself he was not going to let a particular player beat him.

"Yeah, I say it all the time," he said. "But I haven't gone to that degree."

Maddon tried to be diplomatic when apprised of Baker's comments. The reason he pitched around Harper was because Ryan Zimmerman, the man hitting behind Harper, was struggling.

"Everybody perceives every situation differently," Maddon said. "For me, it was about the right thing to do in that moment. It was all about their lineup construction that made me do it. It had nothing to do with competing or not competing. I have to look out for the best interests of us first. I'll never look out for what's in the best interest of the Washington Senators, slash, Nationals."

Was it a shot? Maddon said he respects Baker.

"Of course I do," he said. "It's purely what he thinks, and I respect that."

Perhaps the worst nightmare a Cubs fan could conjure up would be losing to Baker's team to end their season. Baker realized this, but refused to acknowledge. After a long pause, he asked a question, already knowing the answer:

"So Joe is the messiah around here now?"

Baker and Maddon were kindred spirits who just happened to have steered the same boat in different waters. Baker skippered the Cubs in choppy seas and nearly capsized. Maddon had seen nothing but calm waters and blue skies. Both had California in their blood, both are regarded as "players managers" and both loved to talk.

Maddon was regarded by some as an old hippie. Baker once smoked a joint with Jimi Hendrix.

"I'm kind of an old hippie too," he said.

But the two had different approaches inside and outside the lines. Maddon's mantra was "If you think you look hot, wear it." Baker believed you should dress for success.

"Joe manages more like a college guy scene, with the backpacks, how college kids dress," Baker said, referring to the costumed road trips. "I've been more of a professional guy. I was taught a different way how to conduct yourself as a professional. I was taught by Hank Aaron. Not to say one is more right than the other. That's Joe's thing."

When Baker came to the North Side in the winter of 2002, he famously pronounced, "My name is Dusty, not messiah." He sounded different from any of his predecessors, and for a while, it worked to perfection. "In Dusty They Trusty," the T-shirts read, and for most Cubs fans, it was a love-at-first-sight thing.

From heights to skids

Baker guided an upstart team into October and past the Braves in his first season in 2003, capturing the Cubs' first postseason series in 95 years. Before the start of the NLCS against the Marlins, he said he had to "thank God for putting me in the situation to choose Chicago."

But the love affair was about to end in spectacular fashion. The Cubs blew a 3-1 lead in the NLCS, collapsed in Game 6 in what's known as the "Bartman Game" and lost another lead to fall in Game 7.

Cubs fans lost the trust, and Baker eventually went from messiah to pariah.

"That's a shame," chin-beard aficionado and former Cubs starter Matt Clement said. "Because the reason that team was the way it was was because of him, the way he managed.

"I haven't gotten a chance to be around Joe, but I think it was a similar philosophy. I'm sure there are a lot of differences, but the biggest compliment I always give Dusty is everybody knew where they stood. If he felt some player wasn't feeling good about themselves, he made sure that didn't happen. And if I was getting killed three-four starts in a row, he was making excuses for me in the papers, even if they were hitting lasers.

"He's a very good manager. He doesn't deserve the blame. Things happen. It's crazy. When I think back to ... how excited the city was, then how disappointed they were that we didn't win, it reminded me of last year and seeing what was happening."

Baker's next three years could be summed up in three words: Hex, lies and videotape.

Baker said he wanted Bartman to ride shotgun in the victory parade when the Cubs won it all in 2004. The team sold 572,000 tickets on the first day of sales. They signed favorite son Greg Maddux in the spring and acquired All-Star shortstop Nomar Garciaparra at the trade deadline.

Baker was still quite popular, but that new car smell of the '03 Cubs gradually wore off. In a bipolar season full of bickering with umpires, the media and team broadcasters Chip Caray and Steve Stone, the Cubs blew a wild-card lead in the final week. It all ended with one huge, orgasmic meltdown: Baker feuding with Stone, Baker feuding with Sammy Sosa and brutal losses piling up by the day.

Sosa, the sensitive-as-a-pimple superstar, walked out on Baker before the last game at Wrigley Field, lied to the Sun-Times about it and led the Cubs to reveal they had videotape evidence from the parking lot proving Sosa had left early.

Baker never would recover, and the final two years were a blur. He lost power hitters Sosa and Moises Alou in 2005, which he later learned was because Tribune Co. was intent on selling the Cubs, a move the company announced on opening day of 2007. More injuries to Mark Prior and Kerry Wood led to a slow death march in 2006, when news of Baker's eventual dismissal surfaced in July.

Ten years later, Baker says he felt like "the fall guy" for the injuries to Prior and Wood, whom he still had a good relationship with.

"Prior and Wood, that's all I hear about," he said. "Where was my pitching coach, Larry Rothschild, in this whole equation? People think I was the pitching coach, the everything coach. That was one of the saddest days in my life when they told me about Mark Prior's (shoulder injury) when I got to spring training (in '04). I was like why did we just find out when we got there in springtime? Then I had to go along with the lie about his Achilles hurt and all that. They were like, 'We're trying to protect you.' I said, 'Don't protect me, I'm grown.'

"The truth protects. Sooner or later it was going to get exposed."

How will it end?
In his first 1 1/2 seasons in Chicago, Maddon followed the same upward trajectory as Baker. His bond with Cubs fans grew stronger by the day, and there have been no controversies for Maddon to deal with. Maddon said he knew Baker, "but not really well." He never has spoken to Baker about what he went through as Cubs manager, nor does he intend to do so.

"I wouldn't do that," he said. "I wouldn't even do that with (my good friend, former Angels manager Mike Scioscia). Plus, that's none of my business, unless someone wanted to share that with me. Every situation is unique. ... I don't want my take being influenced, good or bad. I prefer my take. So if somebody really wants to talk to you about something, I'll listen. I think I'm a good listener.

"But I have to make up my own mind about things. So I'm not one to call up people and ask them about situations because it's how we react to stimulus that makes us all different."

In other words, what happened to Dusty stays with Dusty.

"Sometimes you meet somebody new, and you talk to five people who might say they don't like this guy," Maddon said. "But this guy treated me beautifully, so why would I choose to take your opinion?

"For me, it's all about how did you treat me, and that's how I'm going to base my decisions. I'm always about making up my own mind. For that group of people who choose to form their opinion based on somebody's else's opinion, I think they're missing out a little bit."

CHAPTER SEVEN
THE METS

Originally published July 10, 2016

Taunting the Cubs never went out of style.

They have been fair game for 107 years and no doubt will invite abuse until they finally win it all, assuming they ever win it all.

Mythical or not, Babe Ruth's called home run in the 1932 World Series was the ultimate in-your-face. But that was just the start. More than one opponent used a clip of Bartman on their video boards after the famous foul ball incident of 2003.

The Cardinals featured a "find the ball under a Cubs hat" video at Busch Stadium that slowed down the hat-switching to project Cubs fans as simpletons.

The Braves paid tribute to the billy goat on their video board in a "Cubs history" lesson.

But a plaque for the black cat?

Few if any organizations would have the chutzpah to mock their rivals as blatantly as the Mets, who have haunted Cubs fans since 1969.

But after moving from Shea Stadium to Citi Field in 2009, the Mets decided to line the sidewalks outside the park with commemorative plaques of the team's history.

Chicago Cubs starting pitcher Kyle Hendricks pitches against the Mets in July. *(Brian Cassella/Chicago Tribune)*

On one plaque on the west side of the stadium, under a photo of Ron Santo standing in the on-deck circle while a black cat crossed the dugout, the inscription reads:

BLACK CAT GAME
SEPTEMBER 9, 1969
WITH THE METS ONE AND A HALF GAMES BEHIND FIRST-PLACE CHICAGO FOR THE DIVISION LEAD, A BLACK CAT RAN ONTO THE FIELD AT SHEA STADIUM, SCAMPERING BY THE CUBS ON-DECK BATTER AND ACROSS THE VIS-ITOR'S DUGOUT. THE CUBS LOST THE GAME 7-1, AND EVENTUALLY THE DIVISION TO THE METS.

That was why Chicago hated the Mets and why the Cubs' four-game trip to New York before the Fourth of July holiday had been circled on schedules since the last polar vortex.

Forget '69. An embarrassing sweep in last year's National League Championship Series was reason enough for revenge, and the Cubs had their rotation lined up with John Lackey, Jason Hammel, Jake Arrieta and Jon Lester. But as big as it was to the Mets-hating public back home, the Cubs downplayed the significance of the rematch.

"I feel like people took too much stock into that," Jason Heyward said before the series opener. "I don't feel like that matters at any point in time in the season. You can get good series out of good teams. I feel like teams rise to that occasion at times, and I feel like that's going to happen here with them. We have to come in and play well. Bottom line."

Not exactly fighting words, but Heyward wasn't around for that sweep.

"People say this is a marquee series," he said. "That may be for TV or whatever. But this is still going to be a good series."

But it was not a good series, unless you were a Met. The Cubs were swept in four games in what manager Joe Maddon admitted was a virtual rerun of the playoff debacle—poor starting pitching, no clutch hitting and nothing but misery from start to finish.

Catcher Miguel Montero, who was called on to pitch in the 14-3 drubbing in the finale, said the players got too caught up in seeking revenge for the NLCS.

That was odd because Maddon had done a laudable job getting his players to ignore the Cubs' recent and distant past, including the metaphysical baggage that goes along with playing for the franchise.

His irony-tinged "Try Not to Suck" T-shirts delivered that message without explicitly saying the franchise is synonymous with sucking.

Whether it was the black cat, the billy goat, the foul-ball dude or anything else fans and media blamed for one epic failure or another, Maddon would not let the noise distract his team.

"It has no relevancy to what we're doing today at all," he said. "If you choose to or want to talk about that, then go ahead. ...

"But if you choose to believe it has any impact on what we're doing today, that's your fault. That's why I say 'I don't vibrate on that frequency.' I don't believe in that kind of stuff, so it's all moot to me."

The Cubs came to New York on a miniroll, having swept the Reds in Cincinnati. Thanks to injuries and roster machinations, the next wave of prospects had arrived—catcher Willson Contreras, outfielder Albert Almora Jr. and reliever Carl Edwards Jr.

The Cubs were having their cake and gorging on it too. They had a big-enough lead in the NL Central to develop the kids and would learn to live with their hiccups. Maddon was loving it, while President Theo Epstein was trying to figure out how to keep them together when the injured players returned.

The Mets exposed the Cubs' strikeout-prone lineup in October, and defensive lapses from Kyle Schwarber and Jorge Soler were YouTube-ready. Did the Mets' NLCS sweep affect the Cubs' offseason roster moves?

"Some of the priorities we laid out for this winter were a reaction to some areas of concern on the team last year," Epstein said. "Some of those were exploited in the playoffs, and to a certain extent in that NLCS. We wanted to add a couple more professional hitters and guys with high contact rates. ... We did that. Wanted to improve our outfield defense. I don't think it's possible to make good decisions if you're reacting to a four-game sample, but to the extent that the four games can underscore larger trends that reveal themselves ..."

Epstein suddenly was drowned out by the noise of jets from LaGuardia Airport and workers with leaf blowers on the field.

"Tell me if I'm not talking loud enough," he said.

No matter.

The focus of the series quickly shifted to Cubs starter Jake Arrieta, the untouchable ace who had fallen into his first funk in more than a year.

Arrieta had lost to the Mets in Game 1 of the NLCS, so this would be a chance to make amends while getting back into his usual groove. Arrieta also would get a chance to audition before Mets manager Terry Collins, who would be choosing the All-Star starter for the National League.

Arrieta spent the first day of the series answering questions about whether starting the All-Star Game would send a signal he had completed the journey from question mark to exclamation point.

"I'm kind of over that," he said. "I've kind of addressed where I've come to this point, and it's a long way from where I used to be. I do understand that. But I've put most of it behind me. It would be great, an honor, obviously. But most important for me is my start Saturday."

By the next day, the talk had turned to Arrieta's photo shoot for the cover of ESPN the Magazine. Photos of Arrieta pitching nude in the desert for the magazine's "Body Issue" were released earlier in the day, and he was pleased with the outcome.

Had Arrieta ever pitched naked before?

"Just in front of my wife in the room," he said. "Just doing some dry (throwing) drills. ... It didn't feel normal, but that was the scenario, and I just went with it."

Any worries about a cover jinx?

"I don't know," he said. "We'll find out, I guess."

For the second half of 2015 and the first two months of this season, Arrieta had been lauded for a dominant streak of pitching that compared with some of the best in history. But now he was suddenly and inexplicably vulnerable, losing his command at times and his Teflon reputation.

Now Arrieta was forced to deflect questions on whether his problems were "fixable."

"We're kind of spinning our wheels here," he said. "I don't feel like there's much to fix. Just throw the ball over the plate."

After the Cubs suffered a tough one-run loss to Steven Matz in the opener, the Mets pummeled Hammel in Game 2, a performance Hammel vowed he would let "disappear."

But Arrieta was ready to do his thing in Game 3, assuring the fair-weather doubters he was OK while showing Collins he was the proper choice for the All-Star nod.

It wasn't to be. The crash came on the first turn, and the same command issues quickly reappeared. A leadoff walk and Neil Walker's two-run homer gave the Mets a lead in the first. A two-out walk to Alejandro De Aza preceded Travis d'Arnaud's two-run single in the fourth, when Javier Baez attempted a barehanded grab of a fly to short center and barely missed catching it with his fingertips.

"That bleeder that d'Arnaud hit was pretty much the turning point in the game," Arrieta said. "Javy made a good attempt. Almost caught it barehanded. Two walks scored again. I need to force the issue, get more aggressive early on in the game. Get deeper in the game. It just wasn't very good."

The mechanics weren't bad, Arrieta insisted. Just throw more strikes. Was he worried?

"No."

Enough said.

The sun came up in Queens on Sunday, and with no batting practice on the schedule and a late-arriving bus, the clubhouse was unusually vacant before the series finale. The Discovery Channel filled all the flat screens, showing an episode from "Shark Week," while Jay-Z's rhymes filled the air on the clubhouse stereo.

Lester, the NL pitcher of the month in June, waltzed through the clubhouse with his headphones on while a song blared out from the trainer's room declaring, "I'll stop the world and melt with you."

Edwards went out to the field to have a baseball-card picture taken by local photographer Steve Moore, who recalled taking Anthony Rizzo's baseball-card shots four years earlier. Maddon kibitzed with the media about bringing back those old bullpen carts with team caps as the roofs, and the first three losses seemed to have disappeared into thin air.

Then the roof caved in on Lester, who melted without stopping the world.

A 14-3 loss capped a Mets sweep that made otherwise-intelligent Cubs fans question their sanity. The team was 21 games above .500 at the halfway point of the season, but another Mets sweep left them queasy.

The debacle at Citi Field was just another chapter in the Cubs-Mets rivalry.

When the weight of 107 years rests on your shoulders, every Cubs story this season has the potential to take on a life of its own.

That's why you can't look away.

CHAPTER EIGHT
THE SLUMP
Originally published July 15, 2016

THE GROWING DIVIDE continued in the first half of the 2016 season, where those who lived in the past frequently found themselves confronted by the silent majority of eternal optimists.

In Year Five of The Plan, it had come to this.

Either this edition of the Cubs was going to blow a commanding lead in the National League Central and suffer the same fate as its predecessors over the last 107 years, adding another chapter to the tale of Gloom and Doom their great-grandparents began spreading before the invention of radio.

Or this was the year they finally would complete the job, causing mass gridlock at Chicago-area cemeteries with fans placing baseballs and trinkets on the graves of relatives.

But here at the All-Star Game, where seven Cubs had been invited to celebrate their own first-half successes, there was really no time to measure the psyche of the average Cubs fan.

Sure, they had become a bit, uh, nervous. A 15-game lead over the Pirates had dwindled to 7 1/2, and a 12 1/2-game margin over the Cardinals was down to seven. It was a baseball version of

The All-Star Chicago Cubs infield during a pitching change at the MLB All-Star Game at Petco Park in San Diego. The players are, from left, Kris Bryant, Addison Russell, Ben Zobrist and Anthony Rizzo. *(Nuccio DiNuzzo/Chicago Tribune)*

"Invasion of the Body Snatchers," with the 2002 version replacing the dominant Cubs.

Ben Zobrist, the 2016 version of former clubhouse spokesman Mark Grace, called it "one of the worst stretches I've had to experience" in his 11 years in the majors.

Since the Cubs had flown into New York at the end of June, when Anthony Rizzo, Kris Bryant and Jake Arrieta let talk-show host Stephen Colbert rub them for good luck during a "Late Show" skit that would air later, they had lost nine of their last 11, including the Mets' four-game sweep.

Curse of Colbert? Might as well add it to the list of Cubs excuses, between the spilled Gatorade on Leon Durham's glove before Game 5 of the '84 NL Championship Series and the blessing of the home dugout with holy water to ward off the billy goat curse before Game 1 of the 2008 playoffs.

The freakout factor was perhaps unavoidable. The day before the All-Star Game in San Diego, Rizzo conceded that Cubs fans "freaking" over the end-of-the-half skid was appropriate.

"Why wouldn't they?" he said. "As much as people love and watch baseball, there's only a select few who really know the ins and outs of what goes on day to day.

"It's not easy, but that's what being a fan is all about. Being from Miami, when the teams in Miami are not good, I'm not a fan. That's just the way fans are, you know? That's just the way it is and we're lucky we have such a big fan base."

The sheer size of that fan base meant the millions freaking out over the possibility of a Cubs-patented collapse were diametrically opposed to the millions who saw a strong-yet-flawed team simply going through a slump.

Talent and resources

The Cubs still had the talent—and the financial resources to add more—to win the division handily and take their chance in the crapshoot known as the major-league postseason.

Last year the Royals went on an 8-16 stretch in September that tested the faith of their own fans, many of whom jumped on board only when the team started winning. Zobrist, whom the Royals acquired from the A's that July, pointed out that the Royals still won it all despite saving their worst for the stretch run.

"We played really bad and I was thinking, 'Man this is a great team to be playing this bad, you know?'" he said. "And we had a lot of bullpen help at the time. We didn't have injuries, and it was like, 'What is going on here? Why are we struggling?'

"There was a lack of urgency because we knew we were going to win the division at that point, but we still weren't close enough to the end of the season that you were playing for home-field advantage.

"So there was a time period when you felt a little complacent as a team. We were losing, but it was like, 'Oh, we'll get 'em tomorrow,' instead of 'We have to win tomorrow.'

"And we hit a little of that in June when we were up by a lot and there was a lot of the season left to play, and we haven't even hit the

All-Star break yet. The other teams played well and we played bad enough that they cut into our lead quite a bit.

"I'd tell fans, 'Be patient, it's a long season.' And we're starting to feel that sense of urgency now."

Zobrist said the 24-games-in-24-days stretch to end the half was "one of the toughest experiences I've had in the major leagues because of how bad we played."

But the schedule was going to ease up with more home games in the second half, so it was time for the Cubs to prove every game matters.

"It'll turn around, we know that," Zobrist said. "But we do feel more of a sense of urgency going into the second half now."

Arrieta in spotlight

Perhaps the player with the most at stake was Arrieta, whose cone of invincibility had been penetrated after a handful of mediocre-to-bad starts. It was jarring to those who had come to expect nothing less than perfection from him, even as they knew it was not possible.

"Look, this is the major leagues," said Arrieta's hardball-dealing agent, Scott Boras, standing in a hallway in a San Diego hotel. "And to me, when he has dominated that long, you're going to have peaks and valleys.

"When you look to the reasons why he has had a few (bad) games, he elevated a pitch at the wrong time (and) your three-run homers and things like that (occur). It happens."

Arrieta was hard on himself, maybe too hard. No one could have kept up that Bob Gibson-esque pace. The self-assured, Pilates-preaching, Texas-loving pitcher insisted he could do it, despite setting the bar so high.

Was the journey to reach perfection so mentally draining that Arrieta now was paying the price?

"No," he replied matter-of-factly. "My expectations are so high that the way I've been pitching lately is not acceptable to me. You want to learn from outings. Sometimes the result isn't completely indicative of the way you pitched, like my last one in Pittsburgh.

"But it's a results-based business. I expect better, and my routine is one that's pretty rock solid. Once I hit that stride and my timing and everything is where it needs to be, I'll go on a pretty nice run. And I feel like I'm very close to that point. My last start in Pittsburgh was a pretty good sign."

Arrieta wasn't just pitching for the Cubs, of course. Like any star athlete, he also was playing for his family, for generational wealth. Arrieta no doubt would become super rich as a free agent when his contract ended after 2017. But if he continued to pitch at the super-human level of August 2015 through May of 2016, he would become super-duper rich.

How high? When Nationals star Stephen Strasburg signed a seven-year, $175 million deal in early May, Arrieta was asked about having a comparable market.

"I'll let you judge that," he replied. "Just look at the numbers."

Two months later, Strasburg went into the break 12-0 with a 2.62 ERA, while Arrieta was 12-4 with a 2.68 ERA. But Boras, also the agent for Strasburg, said Arrieta should expect to receive more when his turn comes next year.

"Jake has a little bit more on his plate," Boras said. "'Stras' didn't have any Cy Youngs, didn't have any top-five Cy Young (finishes). Stras had one 200-inning year in his career. Jake has a lot more on his plate."

Whether it was a "little more" on his plate or a "lot more" could mean tens of millions for Arrieta in the high-stakes game of free-agent starters. Strasburg loved Washington and seemingly took a hometown discount.

Arrieta loves Chicago, but ...

"'Stras' value wasn't based on his geography," Boras said. "It was based on what he achieved and what others had done. He was in a non-Cy Young market.

"All the Cy Youngs are paid above that. Jake is in a Cy Young market."

On the day of the All-Star Game, the "Cy Young market" in the cramped NL visitors' clubhouse included Arrieta, Clayton Kershaw, Jon Lester, Madison Bumgarner and Max Scherzer, whose $210 million deal was obviously what Arrieta was hoping to beat.

Arrieta, like Strasburg decided earlier, opted not to pitch in the All-Star Game, saving a few bullets for the second-half push. The

Cubs, of course, were going to need every bullet from their hired gun to get through October.

No repeating history

As usual, the Cubs also were going to have to avoid repeating history to get to the promised land. The Cubs had sent eight players to the 2008 All-Star Game at Yankee Stadium, providing hope for the optimist that the 100-year anniversary of their last championship would magically be linked with another.

In the prehistoric times of paper punch-out ballots, Cubs fans helped stick struggling center fielder Kosuke Fukudome in the NL's starting lineup, a glaring error that was only magnified when manager Lou Piniella benched Fukudome for the third and final game of the Dodgers' playoff sweep.

Sitting in the broadcast booth at Petco Park and munching on a taco, MLB Network analyst Mark DeRosa, the designated spokesman in the '08 clubhouse, looked at the rosters of the '08 and '16 Cubs and concluded the current model would beat his team.

"I like our bunch, but look at the overriding talent on this team, (like) the starting pitching," De Rosa said. "That's no knock on ('08 starters) Ryan Dempster and Ted Lilly—they gave their heart and soul.

"But when you're rushing out Jake Arrieta, Jon Lester and John Lackey, the 1-2-3 they possess. ... Just to go into the postseason and have strikeout stuff, I don't think our '08 starters could match it.

"Same with the lineup. The only place we would have an advantage was the late innings. Carlos Marmol was unhittable that year and Kerry Wood was throwing some of the most electric pitches I ever had seen (while) playing behind someone. They were lockdown."

So what happened?

Lilly didn't get a start and Wood didn't get a save opportunity. The lineup looked cooked, and James Loney's grand slam off Dempster in Game 1 completely sucked the life out of Wrigley Field.

"I don't think we ran out of steam," DeRosa said. "Over the course of 162, our lineup was dangerous, our pitchers were really good, but ..."

With the Cubs, there was always the "but ..."

DeRosa didn't finish the sentence. There was no need to elaborate.

Either way, his point was that this team was different than the '08 version, just as the '08 team was different than the '84 edition. The only recurring theme that linked them was the weight of expectations.

DeRosa believed this was the year the weight would be lifted, one way or another.

"This team is built to survive a marathon," he said. "This team can do some pretty special things."

As the Cubs prepared to start the second half at Wrigley Field, we were all about to find out, the optimists and pessimists alike.

CHAPTER NINE
THE BIG DEAL

Originally published July 31, 2016

AROLDIS CHAPMAN was nervous.

The 6-foot-4 closer, the guy with the Autobahn fastball and diamonds like disco balls sparkling in his earlobes, had just plunked himself on a well-worn bench in the visitors' dugout at U.S. Cellular Field.

Chapman seemed confident and even a bit cocky from the outside, but the Cubs insisted the stressful moment had his insides churning.

What would possibly make this dude nervous?

Not making his Cubs debut before 40,000 screaming fans in the annual City Series between the crosstown rivals. Not meeting new teammates in a strange town while trying to impress his bosses.

Certainly not taking on the weight of ending the Cubs' 107-year drought.

The most intimidating pitcher on the planet, the Cubs insisted, was nervous about facing the Chicago media.

Chapman arrived in good time at the Cell on this warm July afternoon, ready to put on a Cubs uniform for the first time and start a

New Chicago Cubs pitcher Aroldis Chapman meets the media in the dugout before a game against the Chicago White Sox at U.S. Cellular Field in Chicago on July 26, 2016. *(Chris Sweda/Chicago Tribune)*

new chapter in his short but brilliant career. The Cubs had acquired the Cuban-born lefty from the Yankees a day earlier for four players, including top prospect Gleyber Torres.

It was a steep price to pay for a two-month rental on a team that already had a bona fide closer in Hector Rondon. It was also the boldest move yet of "The Plan," Theo Epstein's much-lauded rebuild, the morphing of the Cubs from bottom-feeders to World Series favorites.

But acquiring the notorious closer also had the potential of back-firing on Epstein, and all it would take was one false move.

Epstein knew the organization and Chapman would have to answer questions about a domestic violence incident from the previous fall when Chapman allegedly choked his girlfriend and fired eight bullets into a garage wall. Though no charges were filed, Major League Baseball leveled a 30-game suspension on him at the start of the season.

In a grim, 35-minute news conference at the Cell, Epstein explained the Cubs had vetted the situation thoroughly and believed Chapman had "genuine sorrow" and had "grown" from the incident. The front office "took the pulse" of the clubhouse, he said, and discovered the players would accept Chapman.

Epstein said Chairman Tom Ricketts told Chapman "in really clear terms we have a high standard for behavior on and off the field. ... He completely understood and was all for it." The Cubs president stressed he would not have made the trade without MLB's permission to talk to Chapman first, an unusual request.

MLB and the Yankees agreed, as did Chapman and his agent, Barry Praver.

"If we had not been satisfied with what we heard from Aroldis, we would not have moved forward," Epstein said.

Chapman knew what was coming too. He sent out a statement through the Cubs that he claimed to have written himself, saying he had "grown as a person" and was "strengthening" his relationship with his girlfriend while raising their daughter.

But the kicker came when Chapman added at the end he would "appreciate the opportunity to move forward without revisiting an event we consider part of our past. Out of respect for my family, I will not comment any further on this matter."

The pre-emptive strike failed.

Forty seconds into his introductory news conference, Chapman was asked about his phone conversation with Ricketts and the Cubs brass. Coach Henry Blanco, serving as Chapman's interpreter because the Cubs didn't have one on the payroll, said Chapman replied the Cubs "welcomed him" to the team and would "hopefully guide us to the World Series."

ESPN reporter Pedro Gomez asked Chapman the same thing in Spanish, and Chapman's response was virtually the same. Three more similar questions, and three more non-answers.

Blanco seemingly was having a difficult time getting the exact question asked. At one point a Cubs media relations official intervened to explain the reporters' question about the call.

"It has been a long (time), so he's thinking," Blanco said. "He's trying to remember. He was sleeping when he got (the phone call), so he's trying to remember what they talked about."

The damage was done, but soon afterward, Chapman had another interview with Gomez in which he suddenly remembered the phone call from Ricketts & Co. Was something lost in translation, or was Chapman playing rope-a-dope with the local media?

Epstein was stopped in the visitors' dugout before the Cubs-Sox game and asked about Chapman's response.

"He went right from this press conference, during which he was pretty nervous, to doing a press conference with Pedro Gomez in his native language, in which he said, 'Yes, they told me I have to be a good citizen, I have to be a good person and I have to be a good neighbor,'" Epstein said. "I think there's a lot to be said about the fact he was nervous and not speaking in his native language."

Damage control

The Cubs later released an email transcript of Gomez's interview to the media to show Chapman finally remembered the conversation.

But it was obvious Chapman's education in Chicago was going be a long and bumpy road. White Sox first baseman Jose Abreu, who played with Chapman in Cuba, believed his friend would thrive on the North Side.

"He's a nice kid and he's the kind of pitcher every team wants to have," Abreu said through Sox interpreter Billy Russo. "The one thing I would say to Cubs fans is they have to be patient with him. He's going to do his job, but they have to be patient."

Chicago, Abreu believed, was the kind of town that would accept Chapman readily if he did his job and if he behaved himself.

"I don't know what kind of advice I can give to him," Abreu said. "He's mature. He knows what he has to do. I know that he has had some kind of trouble in the past, but I also know he has been very good with his family. His history with his family is very good.

"I don't know what happened in the offseason. I think he's smart enough to put all that in the past and keep his focus on what he has to do every night to help his team win games. He's a very special talent, and that's what he had to keep in mind. Just think about his team and what he can do to help the team win games."

Chapman sat and watched the first night, then delivered in his debut the next night at Wrigley Field, throwing fastballs ranging from 100-103 mph and mixing in a few nasty sliders as well.

A packed house at Wrigley for the City Series was entranced by the radar-gun readings on the video boards, treating Chapman with the kind of respect usually reserved for a favorite bartender or a sausage king.

Soon after the end of the traditional postgame dance in the Cubs' "party room," it was time for Chapman to take his first bow. A much smaller crowd of reporters than the previous day congregated around his locker, but Chapman was not impressed.

He glanced at the media mob, uttered "unbelievable" in English and informed his associate and the Cubs media relations representative he would not be talking. Flashbacks from 2004 suddenly danced in the heads of veteran reporters, recalling that contentious day when reliever LaTroy Hawkins called his own news conference to announce he was not speaking to the media.

But Hawkins was a minor character in the '04 saga. Chapman was the Cubs' masterpiece theater acquisition, the man Epstein described as a "game-changer" in the team's pursuit of its first World Series title since 1908.

Was Chapman really going to imitate the Sphinx after his first outing in a Cubs uniform?

The Cubs were helpless to save Chapman from himself. There was no one to talk to the agitated closer and tell him he was making a mistake, that a few cliches would satiate the media and help him move on to the next chapter.

Chapman was not listening to his friend, so Gomez, who had known Chapman for years, spoke to the player in Spanish. Chapman still would not relent and headed to the showers.

Montero to the rescue

Catcher Miguel Montero, a go-to player for the media because of his availability and candor, was answering questions about Chapman's performance and whether it was difficult to catch a 103 mph fastball. After most of the media left, Montero was told the closer was not speaking to the media.

Asked if he understood the stance, Montero said he didn't want to get into Chapman's "business," adding that perhaps the media should "let him be" for a while.

But when Chapman came back from the shower, Montero pulled up a stool next to his new teammate and began speaking to him in Spanish. A couple of minutes later, Montero told the assembled media Chapman would talk after he finished getting dressed.

Montero stepped in and began interpreting, and Chapman seemed more at ease.

"It was fun and something every player wishes for, to come to play and people cheer for you," Chapman said of his debut. "It was a pretty exciting moment."

After a minute or two of talking about being "pumped," Chapman held up his index finger and said in English: "One more question." A local radio reporter asked Chapman if he felt the media had taken advantage of him.

Chapman replied he wanted to "move on" and declined to discuss the matter. The reporter told him "congratulations" and extended his hand. The rest disbanded to make their deadlines.

"Wow," Montero said with a grin. "I need to get another salary."

Wrigley rocked like October the next night when Chapman followed up with a four-out save in his second game, a 3-1 victory over the White Sox.

The Chapman jolt was something no one could replicate. Upon entering the game to a Rage Against the Machine song, Chapman began firing fastballs, making the old park shake to its foundation.

This was something fans could get used to. Manager Joe Maddon admitted Mariano Rivera may have created that same type of energy at old Yankee Stadium, but he couldn't envision anyone topping the electric atmosphere Chapman created in his first two appearances.

"It's so interesting and fun being in our dugout and the place is jammed," Maddon said. "Our fans are crazy all the time anyway, but to bring him into that, and the added advantage these days of having an actual radar gun in the ballpark ...

"Back in the day, when maybe Goose (Gossage) came in or one of these other dudes that threw really hard, there wasn't that gun number popping all the time, so you can only imagine how hard the guy was throwing. Now you know. The overall interest in the particular moment is when you can combine this imposing relief pitcher (and modern technology).

"You know he's throwing hard, but now you know actually how hard, and the buzz that it creates, that's another thing that is good for baseball."

That buzz was evident again two days later when Chapman again entered in the eighth to try to protect a 1-0 lead for Jake Arrieta. But a two-run double by Leonys Martin on a 100-mph fastball gave the Mariners the lead, and a wild pitch brought home another run in a 4-1 loss.

The Cubs weren't fretting. They were ready to win now, and Chapman would serve as the exclamation mark to the Plan. They had spent the first three years of the rebuild spinning veterans for prospects, netting Anthony Rizzo, Addison Russell, Kyle Hendricks and Carl Edwards Jr., among others.

Now the Cubs were doing a complete 180, trading the future for now.

"Given where we are, if not now, when?" Epstein asked. "Given where we are, when those two perspectives clash—the (long) term and the chance to win now, we're going to err on the side of a chance to win now."

After waiting 107 years, the Cubs were now in prime position to end the longest championship drought in sports.

And no one, including the closer, seemed the least bit nervous.

CHAPTER TEN
THE LONG HAUL

Originally published August 18, 2016

THE FIGHTERS WERE in their respective corners at high noon before Game 2,356 of the long-running series.

The Cubs relaxed in their state-of-the-art, Thunderdome-themed digs, reporting for duty on MT—Maddon Time—or whenever the vibe felt right.

On the other side of Wrigley Field, the Cardinals prepared for action in a closet disguised as a clubhouse, squeezed together like sumo wrestlers packed into the back row of an airplane.

Outside of Wrigley, on the corner of Waveland and Sheffield, touristy fans of crystal-blue persuasion performed their annual rituals, posing in front of the Harry Caray statue, taking selfies next to memorial bricks on the sidewalks or toasting the departed at Murphy's, wishing their loved ones had lived long enough to see one.

Just one. That was all they'd wanted.

Due to circumstances beyond their control, Cubs fans had been mired in the dog days for more than a century, while the Cardinals collected rings like Pokemon characters. But with the Cardinals so far back in the National League Central, things were finally looking up.

Chicago Cubs first baseman Anthony Rizzo trots to first base after a walk-off walk to beat the St. Louis Cardinals 4-3 in 11 innings at Wrigley Field on August 11, 2016. *(John J. Kim/Chicago Tribune)*

All they needed was a sign that this was the year. And then came the wink.

As the Cardinals hit town, the Cubs had a 12-game lead and were dealing with the residual effects of La Stellagate, a ridiculous standoff that left their best left-handed-hitting reserve at home in New Jersey.

Tommy La Stella had informed the world, via ESPN, that he was considering retirement over having to play for anyone other than the Cubs. Unfortunately for La Stella, President Theo Epstein preferred to see him playing at Triple-A Iowa, where he'd been optioned despite a .295 average, including an .860 OPS against right-handers.

La Stella did not deserve his fate, but with no room on the roster with Chris Coghlan back from rehab, Epstein felt the Cubs had no choice. La Stella was the odd man out because he had minor-league options. Oddly, the Cubs let him "clear his head" at home, a touchy-feely method of management that made La Stella vulnerable to some of his old-school teammates.

The Cubs had won nine straight, so La Stella's absence was not really visible. But when Pedro Strop came limping into the clubhouse on crutches hours before the series opener, the mood dimmed.

Strop, the designated high-stepping escort of walk-off home run hitters, was an important bridge from the starter to the party room. He'd moved from setup man to the seventh inning after Aroldis Chapman's arrival, but his smile never broke stride.

With Strop going on the disabled list for a month or more after tearing the meniscus in his left knee while fielding a ball in the previous night's game and Hector Rondon nursing a triceps injury, the newly formed three-headed monster was down to one—Chapman.

Into the void came Carl Edwards Jr., the 24-year-old rookie acquired three years earlier in the Matt Garza deal. Edwards, as thin as an ATM card, already had shown his stuff in some big situations.

Yoenis Cespedes couldn't touch him July 2 at Citi Field, looking like Adam Dunn wearing a blindfold. And Edwards had saved Jason Hammel the night before, striking out Mike Trout with runners on second and third and preventing the Angels from tying the game late.

Known to his teammates as "C.J.," Edwards was not ready to accept any accolades and wasn't even sure if his role would expand with Strop out.

"Honest, I don't know," Edwards said in the dugout. "We have six other guys in the bullpen, so (I) don't know what the plan is for everybody yet. Possibly in two (or) three days we'll have an idea."

Maddon had treated Edwards like Waterford Crystal, limiting his innings and avoiding back-to-back performances since a late June call-up. It made perfect sense but limited Maddon's options, especially with the monster down to one head.

When Thursday's game went into the ninth inning tied at 3-3, Maddon called on Chapman, who threw three pitches and was done before his sweat hit the dirt. A screaming lineout to Javier Baez. Another lineout to Baez. A groundout to second.

Game. Set. Chapmanned.

Instead of using Chapman in the 10th, Maddon turned to Mike Montgomery, who got through two scoreless innings. But with Rondon out, Maddon had only Edwards remaining.

Fine china is brought out only for rare occasions. So Maddon had veteran starter John Lackey, his horse, warm up in the bullpen in the 11th to be ready in case the game went to 12.

It wasn't necessary. Former White Sox lefty Zach Duke walked Anthony Rizzo with the bases loaded in the bottom of the 11th to end the game and crank up the Steve Goodman ditty.

It was a gift from the gods, or at least from plate umpire Ron Kulpa. Drenched in sweat on an oppressively humid night nearing the four-hour mark, Kulpa called an obvious strike a ball.

"It's one of those things where it's going our way," Rizzo said.

But was it really a strike?

"I'm on top of the plate and looking right there, so I'd probably be swinging if I thought it was something close to hit," Rizzo said.

An iPhone user in the clubhouse pulled out a video of the pitch, followed by the scene of Kulpa walking toward the long, winding tunnel to the umpires' room.

Then came the wink. Freeze-framed and replayed, it undeniably was a wink.

Sometimes a wink is just a wink. To Cardinals fans with internet-service providers, this particular wink meant the Cards had been jobbed.

Mea culpa, meet Mea Kulpa.

With one "W" in the bag, the Cubs ended the suspense early the next day, knocking out Adam Wainwright after two innings and cruising to a 13-2 win. Fire alarms went off in the Cubs' Thunderdome because of a malfunctioning fog machine.

These were first-place problems, the kind no one could've dreamed of only two years ago, when Maddon was in Tampa, Fla., Kris Bryant was in Iowa and Jake Arrieta was just starting to become Jake Arrieta.

The Cubs were suddenly 14 games up on the second-place Cardinals. Fourteen.

Having grown up in Boston, Epstein didn't learn to hate the Cardinals by osmosis, like so many Cubs fans. But once he got to Chicago, they soon became his Great White Whale.

"It didn't take that long," Epstein said. "All it took was a couple of road trips—they were really good and we weren't—to feel the proper amount of loathing."

Cardinals strike back

The Cubs waltzed into Game 3 playing with house money yet looking for the kill. With the game tied at 2-2 in the eighth, Maddon broke out the good china, handing the ball to Edwards to hand off to Chapman.

But Edwards loaded the bases with one out, then struck out Yadier Molina on a wild pitch that brought Stephen Piscotty home with the go-ahead run. After his third walk loaded the bases again, Edwards became discombobulated, forcing in another run with a walk to Jedd Gyorko.

After watching Edwards fall apart like a sand castle in a tsunami, Maddon turned to newcomer Joe Smith, who served up a grand slam to Randal Grichuk.

Edwards' first failure in a prime-time role was officially in the books.

"Nobody's perfect," Maddon said.

The closet serving as a visiting clubhouse had no white flags in sight before the finale, a nationally televised night game on ESPN. Winning the division was certainly out of the question, however, so wouldn't the Cardinals have to change their focus?

"Change our focus how?" Wainwright asked, staring in disbelief at the ridiculous questioner he'd just met.

The wild-card race. The Marlins, the Dodgers, the Giants, the Pirates ...

Wainwright was in no mood to concede anything to the Cubs, 13-game lead or not.

"They're certainly a bunch of games up right now and we've made it very tough on ourselves and they've made it very tough on us to win the division," he said. "But there's no use thinking it's impossible. We were 11 1/2 games back at least in 2011 and came back and won, and that was at the end of August.

"Right around two weeks ago we were 5 1/2 games back and we blew a game, and they came from behind in theirs, so we could've been 4 1/2 out. That's a whole different ballgame. Now we're 13 back, but it can swing very fast in two weeks' time."

The 2011 Cardinals won the wild card and wound up beating the Rangers in seven games in the World Series. That, and 124 years of hatred, was why the Cardinals were the last team Cubs fans wanted to see face their boys come October.

The skies turned a Molly Ringwald shade of pink as the finale wore on, and Lackey, the Cubs' antagonist without a cause, was in control with a 3-1 lead in the seventh. But then his shoulder stiffened in the middle of an at-bat, forcing him into the trainer's room.

The decision to warm Lackey up in extra-inning games—twice in two weeks—had taken its toll. Lackey not-so-subtly blamed that decision for the mild arm soreness, saying he hoped not to have to do it again until October, meaning the postseason, when all hands would be on deck.

Protecting Edwards was all well and good. But even if a horse is a horse, that horse needs some rest, of course, of course.

Lackey could do nothing but watch as Rondon emerged from triceps triage and blew up in the eighth, serving up a three-run homer to Piscotty and a solo shot to Brandon Moss. A two-run lead turned into a three-run deficit and Cardinals closer Seung Hwan Oh was unhittable.

The Cubs went down without a peep in their last gasp as a few aggravated fans sitting behind the home dugout began to vent.

Willson Contreras struck out and pantomimed breaking the bat over his knee. "Quit hot dogging," a fan yelled. "You're not strong enough and you're gonna injure yourself."

Jorge Soler swung at an outside pitch before taking a called third strike. "You're swinging like Soriano," a fan yelled, referring to Alfonso.

Tough crowd, especially considering the Cubs would still be 12 games up after the loss, which was made official by Dexter Fowler's strikeout.

Remember 2008

Series complete, the next Cubs challenge had a slightly higher degree of difficulty—staying motivated with a jumbo-sized lead and peaking at the right time in October.

Eight years earlier, the Cubs had a nine-game lead in mid-September and cruised to the finish line with 97 wins. October arrived, but the Cubs did not. Swept by the Dodgers—and lifeless to boot.

Years later, manager Lou Piniella revealed his one big regret: He wished he'd told his '08 team to relax more, that no one believed they could overcome the curse, the drought, the eternal Cubness of being.

"If I had to do something over again ... I would've told the team, 'There is no pressure on you guys (because) no one expects anything,'" Piniella said. "Take the air out of the balloon.

"I had never talked to a team like that. But in Chicago, with the Billy Goat (curse) and the fact the Cubs hadn't won (since 1908) and so forth, that might've been a nice approach (to) take the pressure off them entirely."

It wouldn't have mattered, at least according to Jim Edmonds, the center fielder on the 2008 team. Standing in the visiting TV booth at Wrigley, the player-turned-Cardinals analyst called bull on any psychobabble surrounding the Cubs' lack of championships.

"I don't think there was any weight on anyone's shoulders," Edmonds said. "I think the one thing that we might have made a mistake with on that team was I don't think (we) were prepared for the playoffs.

"The playoffs are a totally different monster, and everybody exploits everybody's weaknesses to perfection if they can. It's not the regular season—there's more intensity, there's more at stake. I don't think we dialed it up that year like you should."

Edmonds' claim was stunning. How could team that had won 97 games not dial it up for the postseason?

"Because we were cruising," he said. "We cruised that season and everyone was having fun.

"Maybe the first time you win, you realize there is another level you can get to, another mental and physical level. I kind of saw it coming, to be honest with you. You've got to flip the switch in the playoffs, and I don't think we did that."

Edmonds, who played with the Angels when Maddon was a coach in Anaheim, believes Maddon will make the Cubs' players flip that switch. If not, the 2016 Cubs, like so many predecessors at Wrigley, will be considered a flop.

Over in the visitors' closet, Wainwright was asked if the Cubs will be able to tune out all that noise when they get to October.

"The guys over there—(Jon) Lester and Lackey and (David) Ross—those guys have been through it on the biggest stage there is, so they know what to expect," Wainwright said.

"They know how to carry themselves. They'll be fine. But they're not in the playoffs yet, so don't say 'when.' 'If' is the better word."

If?

Wainwright was assured by someone he'd just met that no one in Chicago was thinking "if" any more.

The Cubs were in. It was a done deal.

"It's very likely," Wainwright conceded. "But you never know. This game is crazy."

CHAPTER ELEVEN
THE ONESIES TRIP

Originally published September 1, 2016

Kris Bryant bazooka'd Adam Liberatore's juicy offering into the right-center-field bleachers of Dodger Stadium, furthering his reputation as the Great Cubs Hope.

The go-ahead, two-run home run in the 10th inning, his second in as many at-bats, lifted the Cubs to a 6-4 comeback win over the Dodgers in the opener of the final series of the Onesies Trip, igniting the chanting from road-tripping Cubs fans.

MVP. MVP. MVP.

It sounded familiar, and it was. Anthony Rizzo heard the same chant two weeks earlier at Wrigley Field, when he pulled off his annual jump-on-the-brick-wall trick, snaring a pop foul before jumping back on the field.

But this time Dodgers legend Vin Scully was behind the mic in the final weeks of a 67-year career, while Bob Newhart and thousands of non-celebrity Cubs fans served as eyewitnesses.

As Bryant waited for his postgame interrogation, teammates shouted "MVP" and David Ross led a Snoop Dogg sing-a-long. This

Chicago Cub Ben Zobrist walks to the team bus dressed in a onesie after their game against the Los Angeles Dodgers at Dodger Stadium.
(Michael Owen Baker/For the Chicago Tribune)

was not your grandfather's Cubs, unless your grandfather loved gangsta rap as much as "Grandpa Rossy."

"Pretty cool," Bryant said, referring to the chant, not the Snoop serenade. "Growing up you hear that on TV, and to kind of hear it now, it's humbling and keeps me determined to do more and do whatever I can."

Rizzo had gone into the night leading Bryant 87-86 in their RBI duel, which had been neck-and-neck since before the ivy began to bloom. Now Bryant seemingly had blown past him in the MVP race.

"I just try to keep pace with him," Rizzo said. "He's really taking off with the homers. It's good. He pushes me. I push him. It's fun to be part of, and to hit behind him and see him do that every at-bat."

The Cubs had won for the 10th time when trailing after six innings, establishing an M.O. that could serve them well down the road. As Joe Maddon likes to say: "Trends can be so trendy."

Bryant compared the late-inning comeback against the Dodgers to a Sunday night win over the Mariners at Wrigley on July 31, when the Cubs had trailed by six only to win 7-6 in 12 innings.

"Obviously the game kind of didn't feel like it was winnable for us, even though we were only down by one run at one point," he said.

"It was kind of one of those weird games. But this is our team, and we did it last year and we never give up. We always believe we can win in the final innings, and this was no different."

The things he has seen

The Cubs had zoomed to 82 wins faster than any predecessors since the 1929 edition won the National League pennant by 10 1/2 games.

Trying to end a 21-year title drought, those '29 Cubs lost to the A's in a five-game World Series, blowing an eight-run lead in Game 4 by giving up 10 runs in the seventh inning, a harbinger of October nightmares to come.

Yosh Kawano had experienced a few of those, and while the Cubs and Dodgers rehearsed for a possible playoff showdown, the former Cubs clubhouse man laid back in bed in a nursing home 3 1/2 miles east of Dodger Stadium.

Kawano was the last link to the pre-World War II Cubs, having started out as a spring training bat boy in 1935 and spending nearly

65 years in the organization running either the home or visitors' club-house. Mark Grace once called him "the king of Wrigley Field," but the reign ended with a forced retirement in 2008, and the Cubs were forced to apologize when a security guard didn't recognize Kawano and kicked him out Wrigley in '09.

Kawano had worked under 37 managers, 12 general managers and two owners. Hall of Fame outfielder Billy Williams said Tribune Co. agreed to the Wrigley family's request to keep Kawano on the clubhouse staff when the team was sold in 1981.

Now Kawano was 95 and unable to communicate, but he was hanging in like a journeyman pitcher who'd lost his fastball. Kawano's trademark floppy hat had been displayed in an exhibit at the Baseball Hall of Fame, but here he was known as "Yoshi" by staffers who kept his spirits high.

Reminders of Kawano's Cubs days were pinned to a corkboard near the room's small TV—a birthday card from a longtime Cubs employee, a Tribune article on the '69 Cubs from the previous October and a more recent article on the 2016 team with the words "Yosh, this is the year!" scribbled in blue ink over the newsprint.

"The Cubs made it to the postseason only six times in Kawano's 65 years there, a streak of ineptitude that defied belief"

But now the team was built to contend for years, and this team was threatening to lift the 107-year weight.

Could they do it in Kawano's lifetime?

If only Yosh could talk...

Hot and cool

Music played over the clubhouse speakers despite a one-run loss in Game 2 of the series, an uneventful affair aside from the bad display of body language exhibited by starter Jason Hammel, who was pulled after 39 pitches.

With a 14-game lead, the Cubs' stress level was equivalent to that of a weatherman in San Diego. No one was going to freak out at the end of a four-game winning streak.

As players got dressed for their Saturday night out, Bulls star Jimmy Butler, visiting Dexter Fowler, proclaimed he was on board with a Cubs championship, even if Bulls Chairman Jerry Reinsdorf also owned the White Sox.

"I'm going to be here when the Cubs win the World Series," Butler announced without checking the Bulls schedule.

Butler was told he could probably lead "Take Me Out to the Ball Game" that night if he was free. No thanks, he replied.

"I don't like to sing for free," Butler said. "Do Beyonce sing for free?"

Is Butler Beyonce?

"In the male form, yes," he said with a laugh.

The laughter cooled down a minute later when the media flocked to Hammel, who clearly was still irritated by the early hook that led to a postgame summit with Maddon.

The laid-back Hammel uncharacteristically held a testy back-and-forth with reporters before asking them not to ask a "ridiculous" question about early hooks from last year.

Was this a blip or a trend?

Mental notes were taken, and the reporters moved on.

Would Hammel and Maddon move on as well?

Ending with a thud

Onesies Day finally arrived, a day Maddon seemed to cherish more than Halloween.

Players would all wear the child-like pajamas on the long flight home, just as they'd done last year after Jake Arrieta's no-hitter at Dodger Stadium.

Javier Baez, the first to try his onesie on in the clubhouse before the game, told teammates they were "really hot" this year. Maddon had "misremembered" the game time, thinking it would be played at night.

But the finale of the wild west swing ended with a thud. Jon Lester threw six scoreless innings, yet the Cubs couldn't touch Dodgers rookie Brock Stewart in a 1-0 loss. Stewart, an avowed White Sox fan, told reporters he respected the Cubs but "certainly don't mind seeing them lose."

The game's only run came in the eighth when Baez absent-mindedly threw to second base on Adrian Gonzalez's grounder with the bases loaded and two outs. Second baseman Ben Zobrist was too far off the bag because of the shift, and Corey Seager beat the force.

Afterward, Maddon protected Baez like SPF 50 sunblock.

"I made mistakes when I was that age," he said. "He made a mistake today."

A youthful mistake but a mistake nonetheless. It was the kind of play that could haunt a team in the heat of a pennant race. But this race had ended long ago, and Baez had been their defensive MVP all season.

Maddon said the players and coaches would not allow the kid to beat himself up.

"He's got a lot of support here," he said. "We were pumping him up on the bench before his at-bat. He'll get the proper support."

The Cubs finished the Onesies Trip with a 5-4 record, losing two of the three series but maintaining the canyon-sized gap between themselves and the second-place Cardinals. The Dodgers' dominant pitching was something to keep in the back of their minds, in case they meet again, but Lester labeled the trip a success.

"There were a couple games in there, in Colorado, and especially today, that we'd like to have seen go a little differently," he said, wearing a patriotic, red-white-and-blue onesie. "But any time you're away from home and above .500, that's always good."

'Enjoy the moment'

Because of the loss, the players canceled the group onesies photo shoot on the field, which had produced a classic "time-of-your-life" photo after Arrieta's no-hitter in '15.

Everything was fresh back then. The no-hitter was still being celebrated, and outside expectations were just beginning to bubble up.

Everything had changed now, even with most of the same cast of characters. The Cubs knew they'd clock into the office in October as the favorite to win it all, and reminders of the drought and past misfortunes would crop up like crows on a discarded pizza crust.

Rich Hill knew the feeling well.

In the Dodgers clubhouse, the former starter on the Cubs '07 playoff team suggested the current Cubs "embrace the moment" because you never know if it'll happen again.

Hill understood the pressure of trying to fulfill the wishes of Cubs fans and millions of their dead relatives. He recalled being at Wrigley with the Red Sox for an interleague series in June 2012 when some Cubs fans came down to the visitors' bullpen with a Ziploc bag filled with their relative's ashes.

Spreading the ashes on Wrigley was the plan, but like a lot of Cubs fans' plans, things went awry.

"They were in such a rush because they didn't want to get caught," Hill said. "The ashes ended up going into the ball bag with the balls we used to warm up. Guys would reach in for a ball and go 'What's going on here?'"

Someone's dead relative was coating the balls thrown by Red Sox pitchers, giving new meaning to the term "Dead Ball Era."

Hill chuckled at the lunacy of it all.

"I think it speaks to the greatness of Wrigley Field," he said. "That's how special it is to everybody and symbolic of the history there. If you're a Cubs player, just enjoying the moment, staying in the moment is the best thing you can do, wherever that may be.

"They're obviously having a hell of a year, so just enjoying it is all you can ask."

As the sun settled over the hills beyond Dodger Stadium, shadows covered the park like a worn, gray hoodie and a beautiful silence filled the air. Stadium workers picked up discarded beer cups and Dodger Dogs wrappers, while writers hunched over laptops in the Vin Scully Press Box, filing stories on the game, the onesies and the long and winding road trip.

A TV near the press box had been muted, but a postgame show was still airing on the Dodgers network. You didn't need to hear it to figure out the team's in-house reporter was giving a Wikipedia-like history of Cubs curses, with an accompanying graphic that read "Cursed Cubbies."

First came the black-and-white photo of the late Billy Goat Tavern owner William Sianis and his goat at the 1945 World Series. Next came the famous photo of the black cat stalking Ron Santo at Shea Stadium in 1969.

The history lesson then ended with the ubiquitous shot of Steve Bartman and Moises Alou vying for the foul ball during the fateful eighth inning of Game 6 of the 2003 NLCS.

Embracing the moment sounded like a good idea, even if the media was constantly embracing the past. That's why the Onesies Trip was a perfect distraction from the outside noise.

Maddon's Cubs had their blinders on, ready for the finishing kick of a season that had flown by in the blink of an eye.

October was still more than a month away, even if the coming attractions had already begun.

CHAPTER TWELVE
THE JOY

Originally published September 18, 2016

THE LAST LAP to the Cubs' clincher had been a long and winding road, starting with a nine-game trip from Milwaukee to Houston to St. Louis and finishing up back at the Friendly Confines.

Normalcy was out the window, as it traditionally is with all things Cubs.

Eddie Munster made his presence known. Umpire "Country Joe" West tried to hog the spotlight. And John Cusack turned up, too, fervently hoping a Cubs' World Series title would not spark an apocalypse.

In the end, the ending turned out to be anticlimactic, like discovering the meaning of Rosebud with 30 minutes to go in "Citizen Kane."

An audible sigh could be heard around Wrigley Field after Ben Zobrist's fielder's-choice grounder ended a 5-4 loss to the Brewers, postponing the Cubs' party plans for one more night.

Taking a cue from Ferris Bueller, manager Joe Maddon told his players after the loss to "just go home" and come back to work in the morning.

A couple of hours later, after the Cardinals lost to the Giants in San Francisco, the deed was done and the division was theirs.

Cubs players celebrate clinching the National League Central Division title. *(Chris Sweda/Chicago Tribune)*

But the team that had partied together all season celebrated apart.

When notifications pinged on their smartphones around midnight and the ESPN crawl declared the Cubs division champs, Travis Wood and his wife celebrated the accomplishment at home with a glass of wine. Aroldis Chapman found himself in a deep sleep. And David Ross wound up on a bike-cab before wandering into a Sheffield Avenue bar by himself for a quick one, only to have the bartender pour him a shot of Jameson, toasting life the Chicago way.

The clinching happened so quickly, with 16 games left in the season. October still felt a long way away, even though it would creep up on them before they knew it.

"It's hard to wrap my mind around it, that you get it done that soon, based on everything we had talked about last offseason," Maddon said.

"Spring training, this season, running through a tough All-Star break, and then coming back on the other side and just taking off. That's really impressive on the part of our players. Yeah, it's pretty incredible."

They knew this was one step on a journey that had many more obstacles in their path, but the Cubs firmly believed in their hearts the best was yet to come.

A good chance

The Cubs waltzed into Busch Stadium for the final time in the regular season with a chance at winning the division on enemy ground. They would have to sweep the three-game series to get it done, but with a 91-51 record and two Cy Young candidates going in Games 1 and 3, their chances were better than slim.

Jon Lester, who had re-established himself as the team's ace, or at least co-ace, tried to get the media to stop patting the Cubs on their collective back.

"I don't want this to sound bad, but we haven't done anything yet," Lester said. "The Cardinals won 100 games last year, so ... no matter what you do during the season, it's nice, it's fun and it's the process and you go through it.

"But what matters here is another month. That's when we put our handprint on the season and what this team is really capable of doing. All this stuff is fun and we're having a great time and playing really good baseball. But what this team is going to be remembered for (happens) next month, not during the season and how many wins and all that stuff."

Zobrist and Dexter Fowler homered to give Kyle Hendricks an early lead in the opener, and Hendricks meticulously mowed down the Cardinals lineup, taking a no-hitter into the ninth inning. But after giving up a home run to Jeremy Hazelbaker to start the ninth, Hendricks and the Cubs made a brief excursion to the Twilight Zone.

West, the polarizing umpire and alleged country singer, thought Maddon was trying to stall when he tried to send catcher Miguel Montero to the mound to talk to Hendricks as Chapman quickly warmed up in the bullpen.

Montero said West told him to go to the mound, then informed him he would be charged with a visit if he did, forcing the catcher to stop.

Maddon went ballistic and was tossed, as another episode of "Joe vs. the Volcano" kicked off. Maddon believed West was acting like the cop who gives you a ticket for driving 35 mph in a 30 zone or the teacher who sends you to the principal for chewing gum. West was a stickler for rules, even if no one else followed them, and Maddon accused him of detracting from Hendricks' gem.

"Absolutely," Maddon said. "I didn't think it was necessary. I mean this. St. Louis fans are really obviously intelligent baseball fans, and the way they reacted to him coming to the plate, I'm certain that had he pitched a no-hitter they would've really given him a St. Louis reception. That was so unnecessary, what occurred. There was a detraction to what the moment should've felt like to everybody."

West was not moved. The rules were the rules.

"Chapman wasn't ready, no doubt about that," West said. "That's not my problem, that's (Maddon's) problem. This isn't about me."

Informed that the Cubs believed West had, indeed, made it all about himself, the Volcano took umbrage.

"That's totally wrong," he said. "I'm not going to let him intentionally stall."

When the teams returned the next night, the Chicago media descended on Busch Stadium. The possibility of a Cubs' clincher was real, and mobs of reporters flanked by minicams bounced from player to player like amoebas in a test tube.

Maddon was his effusive self before Game 2, giving a long explanation of why West was in the wrong. After the virtual soliloquy ended, someone suggested to Maddon that he give the umpire one of his "Try Not to Suck" T-shirts as a peace offering.

Maddon suddenly was speechless, though his grin spoke volumes.

Before the media dispersed, a St. Louis reporter came up to Maddon and presented him with an old photo of "The Munsters," a 1960s sitcom about a friendly family of old movie-like monsters.

The TV characters were shown seated in the Munstermobile outside the fictional mansion at 1313 Mockingbird Lane, and the photo was signed by Butch Patrick, who played young Eddie Munster on the series.

"This really made my day," Maddon said.

But the day went downhill from there. Jason Hammel served up a couple of two-run homers in a 4-2 loss, and the Cubs' chances of sweeping the series and clinching in the Cardinals' faces disappeared.

No one seemed to mind.

"It's inevitable," Fowler said.

Indeed it was.

Ross' monster mash

Getaway day was quieter than usual before Game 3 at Busch.

Most of the TV cameras had gone home because the Cubs no longer could clinch in St. Louis, and Maddon's "Come As You Are" policy allowed veterans such as Anthony Rizzo a chance to show up whenever the mood struck them.

Maddon talked about falling asleep watching an episode of "The Office" after the previous night's loss and admitted he had checked out the first episode of "The Munsters" on Netflix before the game. Maddon said it was the episode in which Marilyn Munster, the normal niece, was invited to a masquerade party of a potential boyfriend.

"When they show up the guy's father is dressed like Herman (Munster), and he was kind of offended by the whole thing," Maddon said. "I forgot about the humor involved. Pretty good."

Maddon seemed to be in good spirits, as he usually was. But over in the Cubs' clubhouse, Ross obviously wasn't himself.

"Grandpa" was one of those morning people who typically made an effort to be cheerful even if it wasn't warranted. He would greet reporters with a loud "Hello, media," which soon was followed by a grumbling "Hello, catcher" from the morning-averse writers.

On this particular morning, no "Hello, media" was heard in the clubhouse. Grandpa was grumpy, and as Grandpa goes, so go the Cubs.

But with the Cubs leading 1-0 in the fifth, Ross cranked a 426-foot home run to dead center, a two-run shot. That was all Lester would need, and he would wind up with eight shutout innings in a 7-0 victory, reducing the magic number to one and giving the Cubs a chance to clinch at Wrigley the next day.

Ross admitted afterward he had a hard time getting up for the game, and was "just off" for some reason.

"I don't know what my deal is," he said. "I was trying to get going all day. I was grumpy this morning, trying to get myself psyched up, and it wasn't working. I felt like crap. I just want to lay down, get on that plane and lay down."

The Cubs flew home safe in the knowledge the end was near. Once they clinched, they would have two weeks to get ready for October, more than enough time to get rested, relaxed and ready.

The big night

After a quick sleep, the Cubs were back at Wrigley for the potential clincher against the Brewers, and the energy on the North Side was palpable. Ross took the "L" to the park from his DePaul-area home, riding in near anonymity most of the trip.

"It was my first time, so I had to figure out all the colors," he said of the different lines. "I went Brown (line) one stop, and then a nice lady, a security guard there helped me—Brown to Red, two stops and it's right here at Addison. I got off, went out this little back alley and the next thing I know I was there. Piece of cake."

Everyone was primed for the clincher, but the baseball gods had other plans. The Cubs blew an early lead, tried to fight back late and ended with a 5-4 loss to the Brew Crew.

Maddon began his postgame press briefing with a shrug. What else was there to say?

With the loss to the Brewers, the hoped-for celebration in Wrigleyville had turned into a dud, like one of those "Mary Tyler Moore" parties at Mary's place where only Lou, Rhoda and Murray would show up.

Police loitered at the corner of Clark and Addison with no unruly "brosephs" to arrest. Bars were half-empty selling their overpriced drafts. "Go, Cubs, Go" blasted from the speakers at the Raw Bar and Grill, a block up from the ballpark on Clark, but few were around to sing.

Ross decided to take a bike-cab home but soon discovered there were diversions along the way.

"The great thing about Chicago—it's different from Tallahassee (Fla.), where I came from—is there's a bar every 30 feet," Ross said. "I kept poking my head in the windows, and between innings I'd walk another block or so.

"I stopped in a bar when (the Giants) won, and I was like, 'You know what? I should have something in my hand.' I didn't want to walk down the street with a beer, so I walked in and the bartender recognized me and bought me a shot. Jameson. 'Rizz' told me it was a Chicago tradition."

Grandpa was back to his old self, and when the Cubs woke up Friday with a division title in hand, they knew the party would be that day, win or lose.

The sky cleared up by noon and the fans filed into Wrigley with a purpose.

Eat. Drink. Pray. Cubs.

It wasn't the healthiest of lifestyles, but it was all they knew.

Maddon played his scrubeenies against the Brewers as President Theo Epstein donned a fake mustache and sat with his lieutenants in the left-field bleachers, watching the Cubs rally in the ninth inning to tie the game before winning in the 10th on Montero's leadoff home run.

Party on, boys.

Dante the DJ spun tunes in the wild celebratory clubhouse, stopping for a moment while Chairman Tom Ricketts was called upon by players to make a speech.

Ricketts had taken a few hits since buying the team, but now The Plan was in full bloom and the championship he had promised Cubs fans seemed closer to becoming reality.

Players listened attentively, plastic cups half-filled with Jack Daniel's in the hands of most of them, as Ricketts took the spotlight.

"All I did was buy some time with the fans," Ricketts told the players. "And the fact is, we used that time for Theo and Jed (Hoyer) to go out and build the best team in all of baseball."

Cheers went up, drinks went down. Dante the DJ took his cue, cranking up the song "All the Way Up" by Fat Joe and Remy Ma:

"Nothing can stop me, I'm all the way up. All the way up. I'm all the way up."

The party was just starting.

And no one wanted to see it end.

CHAPTER THIRTEEN
THE PAUSE
Originally published October 5, 2016

THE AWKWARD PHASE of the Cubs' season was about to end, and manager Joe Maddon already had declared it a complete success.

Clinching early gave Maddon a chance to rest players and make in-game decisions he otherwise would not have entertained, knowing the games were relatively meaningless now that their ticket to October had been punched.

But unexpected grumbling from Jake Arrieta and Miguel Montero over the plan to treat the post-clinching games as a glorified version of spring training had not gone over well with Maddon, who pointed to the Cubs' record during that stretch as evidence they had made the right call.

"For me, mission accomplished this last week or 10 days," Maddon said in his bare-bones office at the mis-named Great American Ball Park.

It was the night before the final game of the best regular season the Cubs had experienced in eight decades, and Maddon was in a pensive mood. He planned to spend the night watching some of the

Dave Wasielewski of the Wrigley Field grounds crew prepares the Cubs bullpen mounds before Game 1 of a National League Division Series between the Chicago Cubs and San Francisco Giants.
(Brian Cassella/Chicago Tribune)

games with wild-card implications on his iPad, confident in his belief the Cubs were ready for anything.

Was it just a matter of flipping a switch?

"No, I think you're just ready," he said. "The momentum of the day, the adrenaline of the day just takes you to that level. You just have to be focused on every pitch, which you try to be all year, but you're definitely there at (the postseason)."

The Cubs had gone 8-3 since Maddon instituted Spring Training 2.0 rules Sept. 19, with one game resulting in a rain-shortened tie against the Pirates, even though everyone knows there is no tying in baseball.

Record aside, the Cubs were anxious to get back to playing meaningful games again, and you could see the nonchalant demeanor in the faces of the players, the coaches and even the writers chronicling their season.

"Of course," Maddon said. "With the players, you have to create your own little adrenaline. The writers, I'm sure right now, are looking for a story, just like our guys have to create their own story for these last several games. And I've been happy with it."

Maddon joked that even the tie in Pittsburgh had some value, referring to NHL rules that awarded teams one point for ties.

"You never know when that's going to come in handy," he said.

Personal goals

The Cubs arrived in Cincinnati with 101 victories and a few goals in sight.

Jon Lester would shoot for his 20th triumph. Kris Bryant was one home run shy of 40. And Kyle Hendricks was hoping to become the third Cubs pitcher in 96 years with a sub-2.00 earned-run average, joining Grover Cleveland Alexander in 1920 and Jake Arrieta last season.

Clint Eastwood's classic western, "Unforgiven," played on one of the clubhouse TVs as players slowly filed in, but no one paid much attention.

At this point of the season, the clubhouse was packed with call-ups who weren't going to be on the postseason roster. "The Expendables" were there to give the regulars a rest, or perhaps to just sit and watch with the knowledge a playoff share would have your name on it.

There was Tim Federowicz, who was designated for assignment in June, re-signed at Triple-A Iowa and called up in September to be the fourth catcher. There was Munenori Kawasaki, the Japanese version of Kevin Millar, who sang karaoke in spring training and took selfies of himself imitating Ichiro Suzuki's batting stance.

And there was pitcher Jake Buchanan, a surprise call-up used for mop-up duty Sept. 5 in Milwaukee and then promptly forgotten.

But a seemingly minor injury to starter Jason Hammel pressed Buchanan into action in the opener at Not-Really-So-Great American Ball Park, giving the 27-year-old right-hander his first chance in the Cubs spotlight.

The Astros had released Buchanan at the end of spring training and he signed a minor-league deal a few days later. Until this day, he was as anonymous in the clubhouse as the team chaplain.

Showing no signs of rust on 24 days rest, Buchanan tossed five shutout innings for his first victory since June 27, 2014, when he pitched for the Astros.

"Not bad," he said. "I'll take it for the first time in 25 days or something like that."

Buchanan would not pitch again in 2016. But if the Cubs would go on to end the drought, he one day could tell his grandkids he got the decision in their 102nd victory, the most for any Cubs team since 1910.

"That's big," Ben Zobrist said, giving new meaning to the word.

No, it was not big in the overall picture.

But Zobrist, who hit a pair of home runs to help give Buchanan that victory, was happy players like Buchanan and rookie Rob Zastryzny, who had made a spot start in Pittsburgh, were able to contribute after days of inactivity.

"It says a lot about (Buchanan), a lot about all of our guys, 'Rob-Z,'" Zobrist said. "These guys who haven't had a chance to pitch a whole lot because our starters have been going so deep into games, and then given a spot start, and to do what they did. ... It was a phenomenal job, and beyond what he has done in a long time."

Though the Cubs seemingly had clinched back in the Stone Age, they continued to celebrate like it was the end of the world. The 102nd celebration of '16 was the type of party where the downstairs neighbor would pound on his ceiling with a broomstick and threaten to call the cops.

Players chanted their usual chants, sprayed their beverages and then made a lame effort to clean up the mess, having bath towels placed on the floor to soak up the mixture of water, beer and whatnot.

When it came to postgame partying, spring training 2.0 rules did not apply.

"Obviously," Hendricks said. "The whole staff, everybody is getting in on it now. It's picking up, I think, a little bit."

Relaxed and ready

Before Lester's attempt at No. 20, Anthony Rizzo and Jason Heyward slouched on a couch in the clubhouse watching the start of the Cardinals-Pirates game and swiping on their iPhones. The Notre Dame and Northwestern football games were on the other TVs, but few were really monitoring the action.

A lazy Saturday morning had turned into a lazy Saturday afternoon, and the end result was a lackadaisical 7-4 loss to the Reds.

Lester said he didn't care about his 20 wins, as long as he got his 200 innings, which was officially a done deal.

"Now we have the real business to get down to," he said.

Lester was slated to go in Game 1 of the National League Division Series, at least in the minds of everyone who had been speculating on the Cubs playoff rotation since late July. Maddon hadn't announced it yet, though he didn't discourage the guessing game, and Lester claimed he didn't know the plan.

"I'm sure when we find out you guys will be the first to know," Lester dryly said, as only Lester could.

Asked about the Cubs' regular season, Lester apologized for sounding "like (a jerk)" and saying the same thing he has been saying all year.

"We haven't really done anything yet," he said, adding the season doesn't mean "anything" unless the Cubs win the World Series. "This is go time now."

Go time? Lester inadvertently was repeating a phrase immortalized by Izzy Mandelbaum, an elderly character Lloyd Bridges played on the sitcom "Seinfeld." It was difficult to picture the Cubs as the Izzy Mandelbaums of the postseason, but so be it.

"Now we have to really kind of live up to the expectation and the hype," Lester said, channeling his inner Izzy.

Lester's apology was accepted, and as the interview ended he gave some advice to reporters for family newspapers on how to get his vulgarity into print.

"Just put a bunch of stars on it," he said.

The end of the regular season arrived right on time Sunday, and spring training mode was about to end.

All players had signed a Cubs jersey with the name FERNANDEZ on the back, and were sending it that morning to the family of Jose Fernandez, the Marlins' star pitcher who tragically died in a boating accident a week earlier.

A notice on the dry-erase board next to the visiting clubhouse kitchen advertised an unusual morning special: grass-fed pancakes.

What in the world were a grass-fed pancakes?

"Go ask Rob-Z," said strength coach Tim Buss, the RoastMaster General who curiously had access to the magic marker.

Zastryzny wouldn't divulge the contents, but confirmed it tasted as bad as it sounded.

"I wouldn't recommend it," Rob-Z said.

As George Harrison sang "All Those Years Ago" over the Not-So-Great American p.a. system, Maddon gave his penultimate media briefing before the regular season swan song.

A reporter tried to badger Maddon to divulge the order of his playoff rotation, which everyone already had assumed was Lester, Hendricks, Arrieta and John Lackey, in order.

For days, Maddon had insisted he would reveal it as soon as he spoke to the players involved.

"I haven't talked to anybody," he said. "By the way, last night, I was watching the Mainers-Oakland game and I wanted to get away from it a little bit so I went to Netflix and watched 'The Office.' This is the one where Jan has the baby and names the baby 'Astrid.'"

As often happened during such moments, Maddon went off on a tangent, going into great detail about the plot and jokes from his favorite sitcom, laughing out loud over the wit and wisdom of oblivious office manager Michael Scott.

When Maddon finally finished his rambling, someone asked: "That's your answer to the rotation question?"

"So Astrid goes in Game 1?" asked another reporter.

Maddon chuckled. The gig was up, but he still declined to give out the information to the media first, as Lester facetiously predicted the day before.

The game began as scheduled, but Hendricks wasn't his usual dominant self, leaving after five innings with the Cubs trailing 4-2.

Still, with two outs and two on in the top of the ninth, Matt Szczur sliced an opposite field, two-run double on a 3-2 pitch to give the Cubs their first lead. Then Montero blasted a two-run homer and ran into the dugout like Jesse Owens.

Lanky rookie Carl Edwards Jr. shut down the Reds in the bottom half, taking a hard shot off his left leg but still getting the final out for Win No. 103.

"How could a ball actually find his leg?" Maddon asked. "How does that happen? There is probably more of a chance to figure out how to land something on the moon than having a ball hit him in the leg."

The final postgame party of the regular season was as super-sized as you would expect. Rizzo even mooned the media afterward, showing off his better half for once.

Maddon had stayed put in his office, trying to celebrate quietly while preparing for the flight home. Instead, his players staged a sneak attack, dousing him with water and thoroughly soaking the office in honor of his 200th victory in two seasons in Chicago.

Ain't no party like a Chicago Cubs party. Michael Scott would have been proud.

"I was hiding, and they wanted me to go in there," a super-soaked Maddon explained. "I said 'No, I'm not going in there.' Then they said 'We're coming in here.'

"That much cold water really stings."

Hendricks wouldn't get his sub-2.00 ERA, but he still would capture the major-league ERA title by a wide margin, the first Cubs pitcher to do so since Bill Lee in 1938.

On the first day of the real spring training in Mesa, Ariz., Hendricks had been one of the few players to walk over to a fence outside the players' parking lot and sign autographs for fans after a workout.

They had asked, so he signed. It was that simple. Back then he didn't know if he would even be in the Cubs' rotation, much less the probable Game 2 playoff starter.

"I never thought I'd be in this situation at this point in my career," he said after the party ended.

Hendricks soon would find himself under the biggest spotlight of his career, along with several other young teammates who had begun living out their boyhood dream only in the last year or two. They all would be part of The Plan, that blueprint Theo Epstein drew up five years earlier and had executed to near perfection, so far.

The weight of a century of losing was now on their collective shoulders as the Cubs prepared for what Lackey had coined the "big boy games."

"This is the day we've been waiting for, to get the season done with," Hendricks said. "Cool to end it on a good note like that. Now we're ready, go home and get a few days under our belt to kind of rest, but get ready, and now we go."

Go time, at long last, had arrived.

CHAPTER FOURTEEN
THE GIANT LEAP

Originally published October 13, 2016

THEO EPSTEIN STOOD in the stands at AT&T Park in the top of the ninth inning of Game 4 of the National League Division Series, staring out onto the field.

Giants left-hander Matt Moore had two-hit the Cubs for eight innings, and they were trailing by three runs. They had blown a chance to sweep the series the night before in a 13-inning classic, and if this dream season was going to continue, it looked like the Cubs would have to get it done at home.

In Game 5 at Wrigley Field. In a do-or-die game. With a city scarred by past disasters holding its collective breath.

They would have to try to solve Giants star Johnny Cueto and his quirky corkscrew delivery, knowing Madison Bumgarner was waiting in the wings to reprise his role as their October surprise. "MadBum" had pitched out of the bullpen in the Giants' Game 7 victory over the Royals in the 2014 World Series, and was willing to do it again.

The fate of this Rockwellian season was hanging in the balance. What was going through his mind?

The Chicago Cubs celebrate winning the National League Division Series in San Francisco. *(Brian Cassella/Chicago Tribune)*

"OK, here we are, now we're here," Epstein said. "Let's see if we can come all the way back. It just felt like we weren't ourselves for eight innings. But it was still there. We just had to find it."

This NLDS already had been a classic by most accounts, starting with the Jon Lester-Cueto 1-0 pitching duel in Game 1.

It was a must-win game for the Cubs because, well, they were the Cubs. No matter that they had won 103 games and clearly were the more talented team.

They still had to beat the best franchise in baseball, the one with three titles since 2010, and MadBum was going in Game 3. And they still had to calm the nerves of jittery Cubs fans who had hoped for the best but feared the worst.

One of those fans had a seat right next to Epstein in his Wrigley Field box the first two games of the series. Chicago-area native Eddie Vedder, a close friend of the Cubs' president, admitted he went into default mode at his Seattle home in the days before the series began.

"Once I landed in Chicago I felt better," Vedder said. "I couldn't sleep, feeling a little tight. It has been such an enjoyable ride and the season has been so incredible, and not only did they win, but they won in exciting ways, in spectacular ways, and with this incredible emotion.

"So it has been a great ride, and nothing would change that. But then you get to this part, and all of a sudden the screws kind of tighten a little bit. But I'm glad it's happening to me and not happening to them. They feel great, just like I wouldn't be nervous about playing a show."

Lester and Cueto dueled into the eighth when one Javier Baez swing sent a ball flying into the basket in left field, lifting the Cubs to victory.

Once the top prospect in the Cubs system, the 23-year-old Baez had watched as Kris Bryant, Kyle Schwarber and Addison Russell passed him by. He had learned to become a valuable utility player, contributing at second, third, shortstop and even first base, using his glove like a virtuoso.

Baez turned the tag into an art form in Game 1, teaming up with catcher David Ross to pick Conor Gillaspie off first like they were perfecting a Harlem Globetrotters basketball routine.

But even after his heroics, Baez had no illusions about the role he had to accept.

"There's no choice," he said. "I was and I am the backup."

Everyone seemed more relaxed at Wrigley in Game 2, where Kyle Hendricks left early after taking a line drive on his right forearm, and reliever Travis Wood showed of his hitting prowess with a solo home run in a 5-2 victory.

The Cubs only worry heading to San Francisco was how they were going to keep Wood from talking about his shot the entire four-hour flight.

'Hard to kill'

The marquee matchup of Jake Arrieta vs. Madison Bumgarner in Game 3 was a case study in cool-on-cool.

Arrieta had a Cy Young award under his belt and had thrown two no-hitters, famously wearing his onesie to the postgame news conference after his no-no in Dodger Stadium in 2015.

Bumgarner was a World Series MVP and had off-the-charts par-tying skills, famously shot-gunning beers after their third title in 2014.

Arrieta's three-run second inning homer off Bumgarner seemed like a perfect harbinger of things to come, but it was just an optical illusion. The Giants chipped away and took the lead in the eighth on Gillaspie's two-run triple off Aroldis Chapman, who Maddon hoped could pitch two innings.

Just when all looked lost, behind 5-3, Bryant cranked a ball off Sergio Romo that glanced off the top of an ad on the left field wall that featured a cartoon dog hanging out the window of a cartoon car that had eyeballs for headlights, and into the bleachers for a game-tying, two-run homer.

Notified of his "car bomb," Bryant asked: "Why do they have a car out there?"

Because a game like this one just had to have a car with a dog hanging out the window so a home run could deflect off the roof.

Rookie Albert Almora would save the Cubs with a spectacular catch in the ninth, and rubber-armed reliever Mike Montgomery would suck it up to get the game to the 13th inning. But Montgomery had noth-ing left in the tank, and Joe Panik's RBI double finally ended it after 5 hours, 4 minutes.

"We're hard to kill," Bumgarner said.

It was a loss, yes, and magnified by the fact that it had come in October against a team that has resurrected itself more often than John Travolta. But music still played in the Cubs clubhouse, and the players were well aware they had lost a postseason classic in an epic series.

"It feels like it," Arrieta said. "Game 1 of the series, and now Game 3, to play out like it did? A tremendous start to the playoffs for us."

Arrieta said the Cubs would "come out tomorrow and be ready to go again." He was reminded that it was already "tomorrow" and that Game 4 would be played today.

"Today, yeah," he chuckled. "We'll get a little sleep. It's tough to not get up for games like this. The emotions are going to continue to run high throughout the playoffs, and that's kind of what you live off."

The Cubs quietly packed their travel bags, donned their Beats by Dre headphones and headed back to the bus that would take them to the team hotel.

"We're all pretty exhausted," Bryant said. "I'm sure they're exhausted too. A lot of thinking involved, but that's playoff baseball at its best. Great for the game, a game like that."

The Cubs never seemed to recover in Game 4, despite an early home run from Grandpa Ross. They trailed 5-2 in the ninth with Moore pitching a gem. But manager Bruce Bochy went to his bullpen, a move that would blow up in his face.

"Getting Moore out of the game and working their bullpen was big," Bryant said. "We had seen a lot of what they had to offer the last game, so I think we were prepared for it."

Bryant started the rally with a leadoff single off Derek Law. The chess game between Maddon and Bochy had begun.

Lefty Javier Lopez entered and walked Rizzo. Exit Lopez.

Romo came on and served up an RBI double to Ben Zobrist, putting the tying runs in scoring position. Maddon sent up left-handed hitter Chris Coghlan for Addison Russell, knowing Bochy then would bring in lefty Will Smith. Maddon promptly countered with rookie catcher Willson Contreras, who responded with a game-tying, two-run single up the middle.

This was a piece of strategy the Cubs brain trust had envisioned during their pre-playoff meeting to set the roster.

"What can I say, man?" Maddon said. "Everything fell into place. We actually carried extra position players so we could burn someone in a pinch-hit situation. So Coghlan gets burnt for Contreras."

Jason Heyward's bunt attempt resulted in a fielder's choice, but when shortstop Brandon Crawford's throw to first trying to complete a double play went awry, Heyward wound up on second as the go-ahead run.

In came right-hander Hunter Strickland, the fifth Giants reliever of the inning. Up strolled Baez, the new center of the Cubs' universe.

It was Javy Time again.

"The game of baseball is a game that is 27 outs," Baez said. "We can't give up because we're down."

Baez singled up the middle on an 0-2 pitch as Heyward rounded third like a commuter racing to catch the last train home.

The Cubs finally were themselves again.

With a one-run lead, Chapman struck out the side in the bottom of the inning to seal the deal, starting the party on the AT&T Park infield.

'We never quit'

"We always yell after games 'We never quit, we never quit,'" Maddon said. "And there you go."

This was Cassius Clay knocking out Sonny Liston in Miami.

Out with the old school, in with the new-age.

Baez would be the consensus MVP of the series, but they didn't name MVPs in the NLDS. Maddon drolly stated Baez deserved a Corvette anyway.

"Javy played incredible," Epstein said. "I'm so glad he had his national coming out party. Obviously we're around him and get to see how special he is in all three phases of the game."

Epstein stopped in mid-thought and corrected himself.

"All four phases," he said. "His at-bats, his baserunning, his defense ... and his tagging. He has come such a long way. So happy for the kid. There was something about the ninth inning the last two nights. Our focus just got brought to another level. Incredible at-bats. It was fun to watch."

Game 4 had fallen on Yom Kippur, the Jewish day of atonement. Epstein could have done a "Sandy Koufax" and taken the day off, but felt he needed to be at the ballpark with his team.

"I think I atoned for about eight innings," he cracked.

As the 106th clubhouse celebration wound down, Epstein walked through the cramped corridors of AT&T to the Giants clubhouse to shake hands with Bochy. The two were old friends from Epstein's days as a 20-something front office executive with the Padres when Bochy was the manager, when he was foolish enough to dream of taking the road less traveled to a general manager's job.

"They're so hard to knock off—10 straight elimination game wins, 10 straight postseason series," Epstein said. "They're the standard bearer for postseason toughness and resilience and everything else."

"To do what we just did in their ballpark is kind of shocking in a way."

Epstein had watched his Red Sox lose a heartbreaking Game 7 in the 2003 American League Championship Series on Aaron Boone's 11th-inning home run, and then saw the Red Sox bounce back from an 0-3 deficit in the '04 ALCS to win in seven games, en route to their first World Series title in 86 years.

As he stood outside the Giants clubhouse, drenched in champagne and reeking of cigar smoke, Epstein reflected on the 48 hours of pure, unadulterated madness he had just witnessed.

"The last two nights were pretty hard to beat, back-to-back games like that," he said. "Amazing comebacks and huge moments, and huge at-bats, and with what the Giants have accomplished over the last six years, and how hard they are to beat in this situation ...

"Our young guys being such a big part of what we accomplished, it felt like a rite of passage almost, that we had to go through them to get there.

"Look, it's the division series. It wasn't the league championship series, or the World Series certainly. We have our work cut out for us. But this has been a special season, and this series has a very prominent place in the story."

The story, of course, still was being written. A happy ending was promised to no one, and the weight of the 107-year drought would get only heavier as they advanced to the NLCS.

But the Cubs were now one step away from where they wanted to be, in a place they knew they belonged, in a time when nothing seemed impossible.

The words echoed again in Epstein's head.

"Here we are. Now we're here."

CHAPTER FIFTEEN
THE PENNANT

Originally published October 25, 2016

WITH ROUGHLY 43,000 FANS roaring and singing and dancing inside Wrigley Field and tens of thousands more partying outside, Justin Grimm thought it was as good a time as any to practice his pickpocket skills.

The Cubs were headed to the World Series for the first time in 71 years after beating the Dodgers in Game 6 of the National League Championship Series and players were scattered around the outfield trying to articulate their feelings to the media.

Always at the ready, Jake Arrieta had two aluminum bottles of beer in his back pockets, waiting for a chance to shotgun. He glanced up to the makeshift stage in center field, where David Ross unsuccessfully attempted to hold back tears during an interview with Fox Sports.

"It's hard to put into words, when you see a guy like David Ross on the podium right now," Arrieta said. "It has been a storybook year, and not only for him but for the entire team. Everybody has contributed from the top to the bottom, and if that wasn't the case, we wouldn't be here."

After the Cubs beat the Dodgers in the National League Championship Series to clinch a spot in the World Series, from left, Javier Baez, Addison Russell, Kris Bryant and Anthony Rizzo cheer.
(Nuccio DiNuzzo/Chicago Tribune)

As Arrieta spoke, Grimm sneaked around the media scrum without notice and deftly lifted a beer from Arrieta's pocket. Grimm ran off with a cackle that suggested he had just stolen the Hope Diamond.

All the struggles, all the doubts, all the hard work finally had led to this moment. The Cubs had done it, and were ready to celebrate.

"This is a group of guys who came here for this reason," President Theo Epstein said. "All the veterans took less money to come here and be part of this. All the young guys, from the moment they were drafted, had their sights set on being on this field to be the team that gets in the World Series and bring it all home."

One more step, and the world was theirs.

Coming out party

Javier Baez's coming out party during the division series triumph over the Giants had turned him from a super-utility player to focus of the lineup in the blink of an eye.

"People might be critical of the fact he can be flashy, but that's something I never would want to coach out of him," manager Joe Maddon said before the start of the NLCS. "Javy has his methods and he's really good at figuring them out, so there are times maybe the method may fail and people blame it on the fact he's too flashy.

"But you know what? I'll take him the way he is."

Javy Time came in the third inning of Game 1 with the Cubs leading 2-0 and Jon Lester up trying to pull off a safety squeeze bunt with Baez on third. But Lester couldn't execute, and Baez had taken off too early, getting caught in the middle with nowhere to hide.

Catcher Carlos Ruiz gunned the ball to third and Baez took off for the plate, sliding in safely for the Cubs' first steal of home in the postseason since the 1907 World Series.

What did Maddon say after that?

"Nothing," Baez said with a laugh. "I'm pretty sure he was not surprised."

It was just the way he was, and the way they all wanted him to be.

"He's probably the most exciting player in baseball right now," Ross said. "As far as how he's energetic, he's not scared of the moment, he stays true to who he is with baserunning and the flair that he has. He doesn't shy away from the big moments. It almost comes out more. And for his instincts to steal home there and to have the guts to do that, that should tell you a lot about Javy Baez. He's a fearless individual."

Aroldis Chapman gave up a game-tying two-run single to Adrian Gonzalez in the eighth, putting Cubs fans in default mode, waiting for the worst.

But Miguel Montero put all doubts aside when he cranked a grand slam off Joe Blanton in the bottom half of the inning to put the game away.

"I thought the roof was coming down from the fans," Baez said.

Blanton promptly threw a "May I have another please?" pitch to Fowler, who belted another home run before the commotion from the grand slam had a chance to die down. Baez cracked that no one remembered Fowler's home run.

"That's fine," Fowler said with a laugh. "I didn't forget."

Sowing doubts

The Cubs were off and running, but Clayton Kershaw threw up a stop sign in Game 2, throwing seven shutout innings to even the series at a game apiece. Anthony Rizzo was in an ill-timed slump, hitting 1-for-23 in the postseason, and .108 with no RBIs in his last 10 playoff games.

"It's the way the game goes sometimes," Rizzo said. "And when you're facing the best pitcher on the planet ..."

The series moved to Los Angeles for Game 3, and the warm weather and sun seemed to settle the Cubs.

"I love Dodger Stadium," Epstein said. "You pull up and it instantly makes you think of Vin Scully, Tommy Lasorda, Sandy Koufax, even Kirk Gibson. There's something regal about this place. My mom grew up a big Brooklyn Dodgers fan, and she was at the parade in '55, so I always kind of dug the Dodgers.

"But no longer."

Former Cubs starter Rich Hill, whose career comeback had become legendary in baseball, was on the mound for the Dodgers, facing Arrieta in his first start at Dodger Stadium since his 2015 no-hitter. Having dealt with all the questions about a Cubs' curse during his time in Chicago, Hill had some advice for the opposing team.

"Just embrace it," he said. "It is what it is."

But the Cubs lineup continued its horrific slump, flailing away at Hill's curveball and looking like the weight of the journey finally had gotten to them. Hill and the bullpen combined for another shutout, putting the Cubs in a 2-1 hole and sparking an avalanche of angst back home.

Rizzo was hitless into the ninth, when his bat exploded on contact with Jansen's fastball and he wound up with an infield hit.

"That's one of the best saw jobs I've ever seen in my life," Maddon said. "Hopefully that does get 'Riz' right."

Rizzo, one half of the "Bryzzo" tandem that helped carry the load in the 103-win season, was now 2-for-26 in the postseason. He blew off the media after the loss, leaving his teammates to speak for him.

"Everyone is patting him on the backside," Epstein said. "It's going to be one swing that locks him in. Everyone trusts him so much. Everybody. It's just happening at a bad time for him. It'll be fine."

At least Maddon was at ease before Game 4, walking down the tunnel at Dodger Stadium and glancing at reprints of old Sports Illustrated covers of Dodgers moments.

"There's Johnny Podres, Zim's old friend," he said, referring to late Cubs manager Don Zimmer. "Man, I remember a lot of these covers."

Bats come alive

Maddon's laid-back demeanor was absorbed through osmosis, so when Ben Zobrist bunted for a hit to start the fourth, it all began to come together.

After a Baez single, Willson Contreras ended the Cubs' 21-inning scoreless drought with an RBI single and the levy broke. Russell snapped his own 1-for-25 slump with a three-run homer, giving the Cubs and starter John Lackey some breathing room.

After striking out his first two at-bats, Rizzo pulled Matt Szczur's bat from the rack in his third trip to the plate leading off the fifth. He thought he had walked before plate umpire Angel Hernandez called the pitch a strike. Rizzo sheepishly apologized to Hernandez, stepped back in the box and cranked a long home run to end his own drought.

"He has hits in it," Rizzo said of Szczur's bat. "It worked."

Rizzo was alive again, and so were the Cubs. Everyone was happy after the Game 4 victory evened the series, though Lackey was still the designated grouch after being removed in the fifth for walking the first two hitters, and took off on the media for reasons unknown.

"We won a game," Lackey said. "We were terrible yesterday, now all of a sudden we're great. It's amazing this time of year all of a sudden you guys can flip so quick. It's funny."

The overall mood was much improved before Game 5 and when Rizzo doubled home a first-inning run with Szczur's "Wonderboy" bat, Lester had his cushion.

The Dodgers tried to get him out of his game with Kike Hernandez jumping around like a video-game character after a first-inning walk. Everyone had known about Lester's issues throwing to bases, and Maddon said in spring training that it was something he may never be able to fix.

"I love the fact he's saying, 'I've had this problem for a while,'" Maddon said. "If in fact it's going to get better that's a wonderful first step, as opposed to wanting to conceal it all the time. It has been obvious to everybody the last couple of years."

The Dodgers tied it up in the fourth, but Russell, wearing Szczur's leggings, stepped up again with a two-run homer off Blanton in the sixth to give the Cubs the lead for keeps. They poured it on from there and flew back to Chicago with two chances to win one game and get to the promised land.

Rocking Wrigley

Beating Kershaw, the best pitcher on any planet, was going to be the key. No one wanted to take it to Game 7, where Chicago would be ready to explode, one way or another.

"We can't focus on the atmosphere outside, or what's going on down on Clark Street," Ross said. "We have to worry about Clayton Kershaw and how to attack him and stay pitch to pitch in our own little cocoon here."

With Wrigley rocking, Fowler started off the first with an opposite-field double. Bryant singled to give the Cubs the lead and there was a sigh of relief. By the time Contreras watched his solo home run in the fourth, the deed was done. Rizzo sent one to heaven in the fifth and with Kyle Hendricks dealing, the only thing left was the countdown.

After a moment of instant karma on Ruiz's foul ball to the Bartman seat in the ninth, Yasiel Puig's one-hop grounder to Russell play that ended 71 years of "next years."

"We'll enjoy tonight, don't get me wrong," Lester said. "We'll have a celebration. We'll have a good time. We'll smile. We'll hug each other and probably get drunk a little bit, along with all these other people here. But we have some work to do and we'll keep going."

After the ceremony ended, the players walked one by one back into the clubhouse for the party, passing the "Embrace the Target" sign in the tunnel.

Out on the field, two trophies—for the National League champs and the NLCS MVP—sat on the stage, unclaimed.

A security guard asked his boss what they should do with them.

"Go get 'em," was the response.

The Cubs had waited 71 years for one of these things, but this was no longer about trophies.

This was all about the ring now, and nothing else mattered.

CHAPTER SIXTEEN

AT LAST!

Originally published November 6, 2016

"DREAM BIG."

Mr. Cub wrote those words on an autographed photo of him and Anthony Rizzo, who attached it to the wall of his locker in the spring of 2015.

Ernie Banks, the Cubs icon, and Rizzo, the young first baseman, had bonded after Rizzo's arrival from the Padres in 2012. After Banks died on Jan. 23, 2015, Rizzo paid tribute to his friend by posting the photo in his locker, a daily affirmation from a man synonymous with sunshine.

It wasn't one of the catchy slogans the Cubs would make famous in 2016—"Embrace the Target" or "Try Not to Suck"—and it wasn't particularly poetic. Just a friendly reminder from someone who never made it to a World Series that it all starts with a dream.

Now Rizzo and the Cubs finally had made it to the World Series, ending a 71-year wait that spawned the "lovable losers" epithet and made the franchise a late-night TV punchline from Johnny Carson to Stephen Colbert. All they needed to do was beat the Indians to

Fans celebrate the Cubs' historic World Series win over the Cleveland Indians. *(Erin Hooley/Chicago Tribune)*

end the 107-year championship drought and kick off the party of the century in Chicago.

Rizzo and Travis Wood were the last of the 2012 Cubs that lost 101 games in the first year of The Plan. On the eve of Game 1 of the Series, Rizzo reminisced about the winter of 2014, when Joe Maddon arrived and Jon Lester signed. At last, the dream finally began to look real.

"It was a turning point," Rizzo said. "I remember saying to my parents 'I should be on a contending team the rest of my career.' The first four years of it weren't like that. It's a good feeling to come in knowing we're going to play this game and next year we're going to go into spring training expecting to win the World Series again, just like we did this year, expecting to win the World Series.

"It's exciting stuff."

It was, and the Cubs not only were ready, they had an October Surprise in their back pocket—the return of Kyle Schwarber, who had missed more than six months rehabbing from knee surgery after an outfield collision with Dexter Fowler in the third game of the season.

A couple of days earlier, Schwarber had been playing in front of 100 people in an Arizona Fall League game, preparing to launch a made-for-"30-for-30"-style comeback. Now he was on baseball's biggest stage, trying to help end an epic drought, with millions of Cubs fans dreaming big.

The weight of the past was heavier than ever, but the time had arrived.

Here they were. Now they were here.

Digging deep

The Rev. Burke Masters, a Cubs chaplain, celebrated Mass on Sunday morning in the Wrigley Field stands before Game 5 of the World Series, as the participants hoped to restore faith that had been shattered in the blink of an eye.

After Indians ace Corey Kluber shut down the Cubs in a 6-0 victory in Game 1, Schwarber's Hollywood comeback and Jake Arrieta's dominance led them to a 5-1 triumph in Game 2 that knotted the Series for the much-anticipated return to Chicago.

The pregame scene for the first World Series game at Wrigley Field since 1945 resembled a Norman Rockwell painting, warm and fuzzy and visually perfect. But the game itself was Stephen King-like, a horrific 1-0 Cubs loss that gave the Indians home-field advantage again.

John Lackey, who ripped the Chicago media for pointing out the Cubs' postseason swings during the National League Championship Series, saying "you guys dramatize everything," was overdramatic during a Game 4 meltdown. Lackey repeatedly lost his cool after Kris Bryant made his second error during a two-run second inning, sending the Indians to a 7-2 victory and commanding 3-1 series lead.

The Cubs' high hopes of ending the drought seemingly were dashed, and the only thing left for the Indians to do to clinch their first championship in 68 years was to win one of three games, starting with beating Lester in Game 5.

That was not happening.

Lester struck out the side in the first to keep hope alive but served up a home run to Jose Ramirez in the second to quiet the home crowd. The Cubs were in the midst of another offensive funk, just like the one in the NLCS, and couldn't find an escape hatch.

Bryant had been 1-for-15 in the Series, making his decision to film a commercial with a billy goat for an energy drink look ominous.

Damn, that old goat had won again.

But the kid with the never-ending grin stepped to the plate to start the bottom of the fourth inning and calmly cranked a home run into the left-field bleachers, tying the game and starting the Sigh Heard 'Round Chicago.

Rizzo then doubled off the ivy in right, and suddenly the ballpark was alive again. Addison Russell's infield hit brought in the go-ahead run, and David Ross' sacrifice fly made it 3-1.

Lester was not going to give up this lead. No chance. But he told Maddon after six innings and 90 pitches that he was done, turning the season over to the Cubs' shaky bullpen.

Carl Edwards Jr. came on with a one-run lead in the seventh, but after a single and flyout, Maddon had an October Surprise of his own. Edwards was yanked for closer Aroldis Chapman, who was being asked to do the unthinkable—get the final eight outs and get the Cubs to Game 6.

Chapman delivered—but only after scaring the daylights out of Cubs Nation, neglecting to cover first on Rajai Davis' infield hit to Rizzo with one out in the eighth.

Would the lack of hustle with the season on the line ultimately turn Chapman into the goat of the century?

Chapman let Davis steal second and third with ease, greasing the skids for his demise, before Francisco Lindor was called out on strikes to end the suspense.

Crisis averted

After the Game 5 victory, Maddon gave the players a timeout for Halloween instead of having them fly to Cleveland for the off day. This was the genius of Maddon, the reason he had been able to get the most of his players. Let them be dads first and Cubs employees second.

There was no way to quantify its effect, but the players appreciated the chance to breathe. Lester and Ross took their kids trick-or-treating, getting their first taste of a Wrigleyville Halloween.

"It was a little nuts," Ross said. "Some lady, had to be about 60, was something. She was sprinting down the street because she didn't answer the door and then saw it was me and Jon Lester walking around. It was crazy, but fun crazy. People were excited."

Another mood swing in the city that couldn't sleep was well underway. Bryant's home run got them off the mat, the tag-team performance of Lester and Chapman saved the season and they had Arrieta and Kyle Hendricks going in Games 6 and 7, respectively.

"What could go wrong?" fans said to themselves, knowing perfectly well what could—and perhaps would.

Rolling the dice

The real curse of the Cubs was not the billy goat or the black cat or the foul ball. It was having to flash back to an awful moment or poor decision-making at a crucial juncture of a potential history-changing game.

In 1984, it was manager Jim Frey going with Scott Sanderson in Game 4 of the NLCS in San Diego with a 2-1 series lead over the Padres. Rick Sutcliffe, the major leagues' best pitcher, was ready to go, and Game 2 winner Steve Trout was ready for Game 5 if necessary. Thirty-two years later, it still rankled the '84 Cubs.

"We've visited that area many times," said Ron Cey, the team's third baseman known as "the Penguin" for his inimitable waddle. "Yeah, it kind of grinds at me once in a while. I didn't discuss it with (Frey), but I discussed it with a lot of people."

Cubs managers, even the most successful ones, had contributed to the weight.

Leo Durocher ran the '69 Cubs regulars into the ground by playing them every day, not trusting his bench players to give them a breather. Dusty Baker watched Mark Prior implode in the eighth inning of Game 6 of the 2003 NLCS because he didn't trust his bullpen. Lou Piniella removed Carlos Zambrano early in Game 1 of the 2008 NLDS so he could save him for the Game 4 that never was.

Maddon had been infallible to this point. None of his crazy moves ever seemed to backfire, and he was not going to stop rolling the dice in Game 6.

Bryant hit a two-out, 433-foot home run off Josh Tomlin on an 0-2 pitch in the first, and the Cubs were off and running. They scored twice more in the inning thanks to some shoddy Indians fielding and pulled away in the third on Addison Russell's grand slam.

Game 7 was not only a possibility, it was in the bank.

All the Cubs had to do was hold on and force a scenario in which the pressure would be on the Indians to avoid a choke. The shoe was on the other foot—for once—and it was a comfortable feeling indeed.

Leading 7-2 with two on and two outs in the Indians half of the seventh, Maddon rolled the dice once more, calling on Chapman again. A five-run lead was fine, but Maddon refused to look ahead. Lindor smoked a hot grounder to Rizzo off of first, and this time, Chapman sprinted toward the bag for Rizzo's throw instead of malingering on the mound.

Two feet hit the bag at nearly the same moment. Lindor was called safe, loading the bases. Ron Santo could be heard from above: "Oh, nooo."

But Chapman's hustle paid off. A replay challenge overturned the call, and the Cubs were out of the inning. Chapman pitched to only three batters in the eighth, and the Cubs scored a pair in the ninth to grab a six-run lead.

With a bullpen full of options, Maddon inexplicably sent Chapman back out to start the ninth. Twitter lit up in Chicago with variations on a theme: C'mon, Joe. Save Chapman for Game 7.

Yes, Chapman had done his job, but at what price? Would his arm still be attached for Game 7? Why did Maddon waste his closer with a seemingly comfortable lead?

Chapman walked the leadoff hitter, and Maddon brought in Pedro Strop and then Travis Wood to seal a 9-3 victory. In the postgame clubhouse, Ross was asked if he was managing the game along with Maddon.

"You're always managing in your mind," Ross said. "I keep a lot of it to myself—what I would do and wouldn't do. I used to talk about it a lot more. I keep it to myself a lot more."

Was "Grandpa" surprised at Maddon's moves?

"Oh yeah, but he has been doing it a lot longer than I have," he said. "He didn't come down there and go 'Hey, Rossie, what do you think I should do?' I definitely didn't see that coming, but I was glad it worked out the way it did. ... You bring guys in in big situations—is he the closer, is he not?"

The traditional role of a closer had been obliterated in this post-season, thanks to Indians manager Terry Francona's inspired use of Andrew Miller whenever he felt it necessary.

"This game is crazy," Ross said. "One thing I do like about Joe is he doesn't take anything for granted. It was pretty cool how that all played out. Chappy, with all the pitches he had the other night, looked sharp tonight. In Cincy, Joey Votto used to say the more he pitches the better he seems to get.

"He just seems to be really sharp, his throwing strike one, and his "slider was decent. He was high-fiving everyone in the dugout, and I told him 'Hey, man, get the heck out of here. Go ice down and get ready for tomorrow. Get some sleep.'"

The Cubs went to sleep knowing they would play in a Game 7 of the World Series.

Dream big?

"Everything you guys write about us tomorrow, if we win it, it will be the best things of our life," Rizzo said. "We have to come in tomorrow and get it done."

'Here we stand'

Armageddon arrived on another unseasonably warm night in Cleveland, and the prevailing thought was the Cubs either would celebrate or implode by midnight.

"Obviously there is going to be a team that's pouring champagne tonight, and there's going to be a team that's disappointed," general manager Jed Hoyer said. "There is no way around that. But that's kind of the way I've looked at it all day.

"Listen, we need to win our 114th game, and it's a good feeling to be able to say that. On Day One of spring training if someone said to me 'You're playing one game to win the World Series,' I'd take that all day long.

"Now we're here, so we have to turn it up for that moment."

Here they were. Now they were here.

Dexter Fowler's leadoff home run off Kluber provided a much-needed spark, and the Cubs built a 5-1 lead by the fifth, beginning the silent countdown back home. Lester replaced Hendricks with two outs in the fifth and threw a wild pitch that brought home two runs, but Ross answered with a home run in the sixth, and all was well again.

Lester cruised into the eighth and had four outs to go with a three-run lead when Maddon opted to keep rolling the dice, bringing in Chapman after a two-out single. Brandon Guyer's RBI double cut the lead to two, and Davis followed with a tying, two-run, line-drive homer to left, shaking the foundation at Progressive Field.

Visions of past disasters danced in the heads of millions of shell-shocked Cubs fans. The ball under Leon Durham's glove, Brant Brown's dropped fly, the 2003 NLCS collapse ...

"Oh, nooo," again, times 10.

Maddon was being destroyed on Twitter for overmanaging, and the Cubs' world seemed to be crashing down.

But Chapman got through the ninth unscathed before a timely rain delay halted the action, giving the Cubs time to regroup.

"I believe the rain delay was God telling us to calm down," Fowler said.

Fox Sports' Tom Verducci reported that Chapman was crying in the clubhouse, destroyed by the possibility of being the World Series goat. But Jason Heyward gathered the team together for a players-only meeting in the weight room and delivered an inspirational speech to get everyone's mind back on the prize instead of the collapse.

When the 17-minute delay ended, Schwarber led off with a single, and pinch runner Albert Almora Jr. advanced on Bryant's 400-foot flyout to center. After an intentional walk to Rizzo, Ben Zobrist answered the call with a double down the left-field line to give the Cubs the lead again.

Another apocalyptic sigh swept across Chicago. Zobrist's double had marginalized the gloom-and-doomers waiting to proclaim "I told you so" after the ultimate collapse.

But it wasn't over yet, and up stepped Miguel Montero, who had replaced Ross behind the plate in the ninth.

Montero had been relegated to the bench since Game 4 of the NLCS. His pinch-hit grand slam in Game 1 of the NLCS was his shining moment, and after he received communion from Burke during morning Mass at Wrigley the next day, the priest was ecstatic.

"Miggy has had such a tough year, and I was just so happy for him to have that moment of celebration," he said. "He deserves it."

Montero had been 0-for-3 in the Series but made his last at-bat count, driving a single up the middle to make it 8-6. Maddon called on Edwards to start the 10th but pulled the rookie for Mike Montgomery after Davis' RBI single brought the Indians to within a run.

Montgomery's arrival was much less heralded than Chapman's, but here he was in Game 7 of the World Series. On Montgomery's second pitch, Michael Martinez slapped a weak grounder to third. Bryant scooped it up and rifled a throw to Rizzo for the final out, lifting the weight forevermore.

The party started and would not end, not on this night. Lester stopped the clubhouse celebration for a moment, and the room quieted as he delivered one final salute to the retiring Ross.

"He went out a (bleeping) champion," Lester yelled, bringing down the house.

The Cubs were professional partiers and were ready to let loose. Actor Bill Murray joined the festivities, interviewing players and clinking champagne bottles with Epstein, who announced he was going on a bender and turning the team over to Hoyer.

Twenty minutes later, Lester stood in the corner of the clubhouse, away from the cacophony, and put the season in perspective.

"This is why I came here," he said. "To break the goat or the black cat or God knows what else somebody wants to talk about. It's over. It doesn't matter. A curse for me is an excuse, looking for a way out. We just played good baseball. We didn't care about goats. We cared about each other, cared about getting outs.

"We cared about playing good baseball and we did that from day one. And here we stand. Everybody wanted to doubt us in LA and say we can't hit good pitching and we can't do this and we can't do that.

"Here we are."

There they were.

The Cubs were finally world champions again, and no one ever would be able to take this moment away.

Ernie had been right all along.

Dream big.

More from the Chicago Tribune

336 pages · Hardcover · $35

A hardbound collection of Chicago Cubs history, told through essays, original reporting, and archival photographs from the Chicago Tribune. Take home over 100 years of Cubs history—from 1876 to the team's thrilling victory in the 2016 World Series.

Order your copy at ChicagoTribune.com